LATIN AMERICAN PALEO COOKING

LATIN AMERICAN PALEO COOKING

OVER 80
TRADITIONAL RECIPES
MADE DAIRY & GLUTEN FREE

AMANDA TORRES, M.S.,
Creator of The Curious Coconut

WITH MILAGROS TORRES

PAGE STREET
PUBLISHING CO.

PAGE STREET
PUBLISHING CO.

First published in 2017 by
Page Street Publishing Co.
27 Congress Street, Suite 105
Salem, MA 01970
www.pagestreetpublishing.com

Distributed by Macmillan, sales in Canada by The Canadian Manda Group.

21 20 19 18 17   1 2 3 4 5

ISBN-13: 978-1-62414-392-2
ISBN-10: 1-62414-392-X

Library of Congress Control Number: 2016961711

Cover and book design by Page Street Publishing Co.
Photography by Toni Zernik

Printed and bound in China

FOR MILAGROS, MY SWEET
MOTHER-IN-LAW. YOUR PASSION FOR COOKING
DELICIOUS, HEARTY MEALS TO NOURISH
LOVED ONES IS AN INSPIRATION. IT IS AN HONOR
TO CONTINUE YOUR FAMILY'S CULINARY
TRADITIONS IN MY OWN KITCHEN.

CONTENTS

PLATOS DE LA FAMILIA
FAMILY DINNERS 15

¡COMIDA DE FIESTA!
PARTY FOOD! 49

FOREWORD

BY JENNIFER ROBINS

Food is a many-faceted, glorious animal. It is social, it is emotional, it is home, it is family. Recipes are passed down like stories that construct our family trees. They become part of our heritage and our genetic fabric.

What happens when those stories, those recipes, those traditions come to a halt because of food sensitivities, autoimmune disease and allergies? A void opens that is not just physical, but also emotional. And complicated at best. Older generations are insulted and younger generations sad at the thought of being unable to take part in family traditions.

Paleo eaters find the lifestyle for a variety of reasons, many seeking for optimal health and well-being. Some, however, are required to eat grain-, dairy- and sugar-free to curb inflammation caused by the "standard" way of eating. Eating this way is a lifesaver for many and can help restore normalcy to those who are suffering. The struggle comes when cultural food norms must be abandoned in order to adhere to more healthful choices.

Amanda Torres, of The Curious Coconut, knows all too well about sacrificing favorite foods, and about those that felt like home. Through her own struggles with obesity and health issues, Amanda knew there was no other choice than to turn away from "comfort" foods and embrace those that were nutrient-dense and healing.

But Amanda wanted to embrace traditional foods, too, especially the beloved Puerto Rican recipes from her husband's family that she adored so much. She began using her blog, The Curious Coconut, to find creative ways to recreate these recipes, making them without such grains as wheat and corn, and without dairy as well. Then, after moving to Miami, Florida, she realized that there were endless recipes from other parts of Latin America she wanted to recreate: Cuban, Colombian, Venezuelan, Peruvian, Brazilian and Argentinean, among others.

In these pages, you'll find Amanda's whole-hearted, whole-food approach to embracing Latin American foods, making them completely grain-, gluten-, dairy- and refined sugar–free. She's included everything from empanadas to Peruvian chicken to *papas rellenas* to *chicharrónes* to *pupusas*. Collaborating with her mother-in-law, she's placed a special emphasis on Puerto Rican dishes, using recipes passed down for generations for *pasteles*, *alcapurrias*, *bacalaitos* and more. She has seasonings, sauces, sides, sweets and everything in between. I know that Amanda dedicates herself entirely to make certain that when she is writing a new recipe, it is not only authentic, but soulfully connected to the original recipe she is recreating. And as a fan of Latin fare, I'm equally as excited to dive into the recipes to include in my own kitchen.

I got to meet Amanda in person at Joel Salatin's Polyface Farm, which exemplifies ethical and sustainable farming. We connected there over a shared dedication to using high-quality and humanely produced food as medicine. At the time, there were very few resources for those trying to navigate autoimmune disease and diet, and we got to know each other better as we grew our websites to help fill that void. Amanda has taken care not to exclude the autoimmune community with this cookbook, providing many substitutions so that those who need to avoid nightshades, nuts, eggs and seeds can still enjoy delicious Latin American food.

In short, roll your sleeves up, put on some music and dig into *Latin American Paleo Cooking*. You'll begin to hear the stories of generations past, inhale the fragrant history of the recipes and taste the love poured into each dish. *¡Buen provecho!*

INTRODUCTION

¡Hola! My name is Amanda Torres, founder of the blog The Curious Coconut, a trusted source for delicious and creative grain-free, dairy-free, allergy-friendly food suitable for the Paleo diet as well as the autoimmune protocol. I am awed and extremely grateful to be presenting this cookbook to you, something I never would have thought possible until just a few years ago.

I am from a relatively small town in the middle of Georgia and had very little exposure to other cultures growing up. I was raised to have a deep respect for food, especially recipes passed down for generations within the family. Even though I was an extremely picky eater growing up, when I moved to New Orleans to earn my BS and MS degrees in neuroscience, I embraced the unique local cuisine.

I was first introduced to Puerto Rican cuisine in 2005, when I met my future husband, Andy, whose parents are both from the island. Andy and I both adopted the Paleo diet in 2010 because I was obese and facing numerous health problems, including hypertension, prediabetes, depression and an autoimmune skin condition called hidradenitis suppurativa. One year later, I had lost 80 pounds and no longer needed any prescription or over-the-counter medications and had healed or put everything into remission.

In 2012 we moved to Miami Beach to a neighborhood known as Little Argentina. I was eager to learn everything I could about the new dining options that had suddenly opened up to me, which included Peruvian, Cuban, Brazilian, Argentinean, Venezuelan and Colombian restaurants. My co-workers at the University of Miami Medical School were primarily all originally from a Latin American country. Finding myself so immersed in such a diverse array of Latin American cultures, I embraced all of the new foods I was exposed to. Something that really struck me is that so much of the food was, by its very nature, very Paleo friendly. In many cases, all you had to do was ensure you were using a healthy cooking fat and the dish was perfectly compliant.

And so my passion for sharing traditional Latin American food with the Paleo community was born. Ever since the inception of my blog in 2012, I have always loved to educate about the traditional ingredients (such as plantains, yuca and malanga) and share authentic recipes.

I have also made it a point to spend as much time in the kitchen as possible every time we visit my dear sweet mother-in-law, Milagros. She is an incredible cook and has so graciously shared her heirloom family recipes with me to include in this cookbook. I have learned so much from her over the years!

While all of the recipes are written to be Paleo, I have also taken care to include directions for substitutions to make as many recipes as possible autoimmune protocol (AIP) compliant. I spent the better part of a year on the AIP working to heal leaky gut syndrome, with which I was diagnosed in 2014. The AIP goes beyond Paleo, which excludes grains, legumes and dairy, to further remove other potentially inflammatory foods: eggs, nightshades (peppers, eggplant, tomatoes, potatoes, etc.), nuts and seeds.

If you have found yourself bored with the same ol' recipes in your Paleo diet, or have been pining for Paleo-friendly versions of your favorite Latin dishes, this cookbook is for you. The layers of flavor in these recipes will open your palate up to a whole new experience and help keep the Paleo diet fresh and exciting for you.

¡Buen provecho!

Amanda

NOTE: Before you get started, you may want to read my primer on special ingredients (page 177) and learn more about the cooking basics (page 173).

PLATOS DE LA FAMILIA

FAMILY DINNERS

In Milagros's family, as is typical in Latin American culture, the family dinner at the end of each day is the most important meal. Whereas breakfast and lunch may be served as small portions, eaten alone or even eaten on the go, dinner is the main event each day. It is the one meal that the entire family can expect to be hearty, filling, comforting and shared with loved ones.

This is actually how I was raised to treat dinnertime, too, growing up in the South in the United States. Unfortunately, in today's world full of digital distractions, the family dinner is slowly disappearing. Reclaim it with the hearty meals in this chapter, which feature beloved traditional dishes meant to feed a crowd. Many of these recipes are excellent for batch cooking and freezing for later, so that even on the busiest weeknights you can have something exciting on hand to thaw and enjoy together with your family. I've also made every effort to make the more time-consuming dishes faster and easier to prepare without sacrificing the authenticity of flavor, and to provide slow cooker directions, too. *¡Buen provecho!*

Pasteles, recipe on page 33.

MILAGROS'S FAMOUS PERNIL AL HORNO

ADOBO MOJADO MARINATED PORK ROAST

 Puerto Rico

The flavor that this seasoning blend, called *adobo*, imparts into the pork roast is absolutely incredible. This is Milagros's famous pork roast recipe that family always requests when visiting her. It is especially popular during the holiday season and can make a great alternative to cured ham if you're looking for something new and exciting. Scale the recipe up to accommodate a whole shoulder roast or fresh ham and start a new tradition!

SERVES 4 TO 6

2 tbsp (20 g) minced garlic (about 1 whole head)

1½ tsp (9 g) fine Himalayan salt

1½ tsp (3 g) dried oregano

1 tsp (2 g) freshly ground black pepper

½ tsp ground turmeric

1 tsp (2 g) ground coriander seeds

1½ tbsp (25 ml) extra-virgin olive oil

1½ tbsp (25 ml) freshly squeezed lime juice

1 (4- to 5-lb [1.8- to 2.3-kg]) bone-in pork shoulder roast

In a small bowl, combine all the ingredients, except the pork, to form a paste.

Cut slits in the skin on the top of the roast and pierce all sides of the roast with a knife to help the seasoning blend penetrate the meat. Coat the roast with the paste and place in a large resealable plastic bag or wrap it in a few layers of plastic wrap. Allow to marinate overnight, up to 24 hours.

Before roasting, remove the pork from the refrigerator and allow to stand at room temperature for 30 minutes. Preheat the oven to 400°F (200°C).

Remove the wrappings from the pork. Roast the pork for 1 hour, uncovered and skin side up, in a pan with sides a few inches tall to accommodate all the fat that will render out during roasting. Then, without opening the oven, lower the temperature to 300°F (150°C) and continue to roast until a meat thermometer inserted into the thickest part of the roast (not touching the bone) reads 185°F (85°C), or for 2 to 3 hours longer (40 to 45 minutes per pound [455 g] of roast). You may wish to check the roast after 1½ hours' roasting at 300°F (150°C).

The roast is done when the meat shreds easily with a fork and the fat on top is nicely crisped.

AIP COMPLIANT: Omit the black pepper and coriander seeds from the *adobo*.

VACA FRITA

GARLIC-LIME FRIED SHREDDED BEEF

 Cuba

Vaca frita literally means "fried cow" and is, hands-down, my favorite Cuban dish. Some real culinary magic happens when you take slow-cooked beef, season it intensely with garlic and lime and then fry it until it achieves this tantalizing crispy-on-the-outside yet delightfully tender-on-the-inside texture.

SERVES 4 TO 6

FOR THE STEAK

2 lb (905 g) flank steak

1 onion, quartered

1 bell pepper, stemmed, seeded and quartered

2 cloves garlic, crushed

1 bay leaf

6 black peppercorns

FOR SEASONING

1 tbsp (10 g) minced garlic

2 tsp (12 g) fine Himalayan salt

Juice of 1 to 2 limes

FOR FRYING

About ¼ cup (56 g) lard, avocado oil or extra-virgin olive oil, divided

1 large white onion, sliced thickly, divided

2 limes, cut into wedges

Chopped fresh cilantro, for garnish (optional)

To prepare the steak, cut it crosswise into 2 or 3 pieces and place in a large pot. Add the quartered onion, bell pepper, garlic, bay leaf and peppercorns and cover everything with water. Bring to a boil over high heat, then cover and lower the heat to a moderate simmer. Cook until the steak is falling-apart tender, 2½ to 3 hours.

Remove the steak from the pot and shred with 2 forks. Strain the broth and reserve for another use, discarding the cooked onion, bell pepper, bay leaf and peppercorns.

To season the steak, combine the shredded steak with the seasoning ingredients in a bowl. Tip: You can leave the cooked shredded meat in the seasoning, refrigerated, for several hours or overnight. It will make the meat more flavorful, but is not necessary. If you do batch cooking, you can actually leave it in the marinade for up to 3 days, frying it up fresh each time you eat a portion.

To fry the steak, work in batches to fry the meat. In a large skillet, heat about 2 tablespoons (28 g) of your fat of choice over medium heat for 3 to 4 minutes. Add the meat shreds to the pan without crowding them to ensure that the meat fries and does not steam. Spread out the meat with spacing throughout. Allow it to fry for 5 to 8 minutes, stirring a few times. Add about one-third of the sliced onion and continue to fry until the onion has softened, 3 to 5 minutes. Transfer the mixture to a serving plate and keep warm. Continue until all the meat and onion is cooked.

Serve with lime wedges and garnish with cilantro, if desired.

NOTES: For a less hands-on cooking method, place all the ingredients for the steak in a slow cooker and cook on low for about 8 hours, shred the meat, then finish cooking as directed.

Although flank steak is the traditional cut used, thanks to the pronounced look of the shreds once cooked, you may also substitute a chuck roast, which usually weighs about 4 pounds (1.8 kg). Double the remaining ingredients and increase the cooking time to 3 to 4 hours for tender, fork-shreddable chuck. Or, put it all in the slow cooker as described above.

AIP COMPLIANT: Simply omit the bell pepper and peppercorns from the first step.

LOMO SALTADO

STEAK AND FRENCH FRY STIR-FRY

 Peru

Lomo saltado is a fusion of Chinese and Peruvian cuisine, which arose as a result of indentured Chinese workers coming to Peru in the mid-1800s and introducing stir-frying and soy sauce to the region. The flavors and textures in this dish, with the quick-seared steak, spicy peppers and crispy fried potatoes, are sure to delight your senses and quickly turn this into a new household favorite. For a strictly Paleo version, use coconut aminos to replace the soy sauce, but note that using gluten-free tamari will result in a bolder flavor.

SERVES 2

FOR THE POTATOES

1 lb (455 g) russet potatoes (about 4 medium potatoes)

About ½ cup (112 g) fat for frying (lard or duck fat recommended), or if oven-roasting, 2 tbsp (30 ml) melted fat to coat the fries

Fine Himalayan salt, to taste

FOR THE MEAT

1 lb (455 g) trimmed sirloin steak, cut into slices ½" (1.3 cm) thick and about 2" (5 cm) long

1 tbsp (15 ml) coconut aminos (or gluten-free tamari if you tolerate soy)

2 large cloves garlic, minced

½ tsp fine Himalayan salt

½ tsp freshly ground black pepper

4 tbsp (60 ml) avocado oil for frying (avocado is the only Paleo oil suitable for frying at such high temperatures)

To prepare the potatoes, peel and cut them lengthwise into sticks ½ inch (1.3 cm) thick, then place the sticks in a large bowl. Cover with water and let sit for at least 20 minutes. Drain and pat dry. Soaking the potatoes like this before frying is the secret to french fries that are tender on the inside and crispy on the outside. If frying the potatoes, melt the fat in a large skillet over medium heat for 4 to 5 minutes. Working in batches if necessary, carefully drop the potato sticks into the fat and cook, turning once or twice during frying, until golden brown and crispy, 20 to 25 minutes. Drain on a paper towel–lined plate and season to taste with salt.

If oven-roasting, preheat the oven to 450°F (230°C). Soak and drain as directed for frying, then coat with the melted fat and salt. Arrange the fries in a single layer on a rimmed baking sheet and bake for 25 to 35 minutes, flipping once halfway through for even cooking.

To prepare the meat, combine the strips of steak and all the meat ingredients, except the avocado oil, in a bowl and toss well. In a large skillet or wok, heat the avocado oil over high heat for 2 to 3 minutes. Cook the meat in batches as necessary; do not overcrowd the meat in the pan. Rapidly stir-fry the meat for 3 to 5 minutes, until both sides are seared. Remove with a slotted spoon and set aside.

(continued)

FOR THE VEGETABLES

2 to 3 cloves garlic, peeled and minced

1 red onion, thickly sliced

1 to 2 *ajíes amarillos* (sold frozen or dried at some Latin American markets), or jalapeño or serrano peppers, stemmed and seeded and sliced thinly (if you prefer a nonspicy dish, substitute 1 yellow bell pepper)

3 plum tomatoes, cut into wedges

4 tbsp (60 ml) coconut aminos (or gluten-free tamari if you tolerate soy)

1 tbsp (15 ml) coconut vinegar or white wine vinegar

¼ cup (4 g) chopped fresh cilantro

To prepare the vegetables, using the same skillet, lower the heat to medium and add the garlic, stirring quickly for 10 to 20 seconds, then add the red onion, quickly stir-frying for 2 to 3 minutes. Add the *ajíes amarillos* and cook for 1 to 2 more minutes. Remove everything with a slotted spoon and set aside. Add the tomato wedges and cook, stirring frequently, for 2 to 3 minutes.

Increase the heat back to high and return the reserved vegetables and meat to the pan. Stir in the coconut aminos and vinegar. Cook, stirring frequently, for 2 to 3 minutes. Turn off the heat and stir in the cilantro. Just before serving, add the potatoes, stirring to combine with the meat and juices. Serve immediately. Traditionally paired with white rice, which you can replace with the "Arroz" Blanco o Amarillo de Malanga (page 118).

AIP COMPLIANT: Use coconut aminos and omit the peppers and tomatoes, optionally replacing them with zucchini slices and/or extra onion. Use Yuca Frita (page 124) in place of the potato fries.

PIÑON/PASTELÓN
RIPE PLANTAIN LASAGNA OR MEAT PIE

 *Puerto Rico & Dominican Republic*

Piñon and *pastelón* are two variations of a similar casserole made with ripe plantains and ground beef. Depending on where in Puerto Rico or the Dominican Republic you are, the names can be used interchangeably or even reversed. It can be confusing. One features ripe plantains cut into strips, fried and layered like lasagna. The other features mashed ripe plantains turned into a pie crust. In Milagros's family, they call the plantain lasagna version *pastelón*, but other Puerto Ricans call it *piñon*. Either way, they are both delicious and perfect for feeding a crowd. The lasagna version is not AIP-friendly but the crust version is!

SERVES 8

FOR PLANTAIN LASAGNA

6 ripe plantains

¼ cup (56 g) lard, coconut oil or avocado oil for frying, plus more as needed

1½ lb (680 g) ground beef

4 tbsp (55 g) Sofrito (page 148)

1 onion, diced

1 red bell pepper, diced

1½ tsp (3 g) dried oregano

2¼ tsp (11 g) fine Himalayan salt, divided

2 tbsp (13 g) sliced green olives

2 tsp (6 g) drained capers

Juice of 1 lime

6 large eggs, beaten

Prepare the lasagna: Preheat the oven to 350°F (180°C).

To peel ripe plantains, first slice off both tips with a knife, then cut a slit in the skin down the length of the plantain. Lift off the peel with your fingers. Cut each plantain lengthwise into strips about ½ inch (1.3 cm) thick. Aim for getting 5 slices per plantain.

In a large skillet, heat your fat of choice over medium heat until shimmering, 3 to 5 minutes. Carefully arrange the plantain slices in a single layer in the skillet and cook until lightly browned on both sides, 3 to 5 minutes per side. Drain on a paper towel–lined plate, cooking the remaining plantains in batches until all the strips are cooked. Try to keep them whole, but it's okay if some of them break apart during cooking.

Meanwhile, in a second large skillet, you can cook the meat filling while the plantains are frying. Place the ground beef and *sofrito* in the pan and cook over medium heat until the meat is about three-quarters of the way browned, about 10 minutes. Add the onion and bell pepper and cook until the meat is fully browned, about 5 more minutes. Stir in the oregano, 1½ teaspoons (9 g) of the salt and the olives, capers and lime juice. Lower the heat to low and cook until the plantain slices in the other pan are all cooked.

To assemble the lasagna, grease a large baking dish (9 x 13 inches [23 x 33 cm], at least 2 inches [5 cm] deep). Beat the eggs and the remaining ¾ teaspoon of salt with a whisk and pour half of this mixture into the bottom of the prepared pan. Arrange the fried plantain slices in a single layer across the bottom of the dish, using whole strips if possible. Save any broken strips for the middle layer. You should need 9 to 10 strips per layer. Next, add half of the ground meat mixture and spread evenly. Add another layer of plantains (using up any broken strips), then the remaining meat mixture, and finish it off with the top layer of plantain, using whole slices if possible for presentation. Pour the remaining beaten egg mixture evenly on top of the casserole.

Bake for 30 minutes, or until the egg is set and top of the casserole is golden brown. Allow to rest about 5 minutes before serving. Divide into 8 square servings and enjoy!

(continued)

ADJUSTMENTS FOR THE PLANTAIN CRUST VERSION

¼ cup (30 g) sifted cassava flour

¼ cup (60 g) lard or coconut oil

1 tsp (6 g) fine Himalayan salt

For the crust version, after peeling the plantains, place them in a pot and cover with water. Boil until fork-tender, 15 to 20 minutes. Drain and mash with the cassava flour, fat of choice and the salt. Grease a 9 x 13-inch (23 x 33-cm) baking dish and spread about half of the plantain mash across the bottom and up the sides. Fill with the meat mixture, then cover with the remaining plantain mash (you can roll the remaining mash into small balls and flatten between your hands, arranging these pieces side by side, then smoothing the seams together with your fingers).

Bake for 30 minutes at 350°F (180°C) and allow to rest for about 5 minutes before serving.

AIP COMPLIANT: Make the crust version, omitting the red bell pepper from the meat mixture. Or simply use the AIP-compliant version of Carne Molida (page 95).

POLLO A LA BRASA
MARINATED ROASTED CHICKEN

 Peru

Pollo a la brasa is a flavorful marinated roasted chicken recipe that is traditionally cooked in a rotisserie, but that you can roast in your oven with excellent results. Thanks to the rich marinade, the skin is very well seasoned and turns out extra crispy. Be aware that restaurants may use beer and/or soy sauce (which contains gluten) so be sure to ask about the marinade if you ever dine at a Peruvian restaurant.

SERVES 2 TO 4

2 tbsp (30 ml) coconut aminos (or gluten-free tamari if you tolerate soy)

1 tbsp (10 g) minced garlic

1 tbsp (14 g) *huacatay* paste (also known as black mint)

½ tsp fine Himalayan salt

¼ tsp freshly ground black pepper

½ tsp dried oregano

1 tbsp (15 g) *ají panca* paste

1 tbsp (14 ml) extra-virgin olive oil

Juice of 1 lime

1 (3- to 4-lb [1.4- to 1.8-kg]) whole chicken

In a small bowl, combine all the ingredients except the chicken to create a marinade. Remove the giblets from the cavity of the chicken and gently separate the skin from the breast and from the thighs. Rub some of the marinade underneath the skin and use the rest to generously cover the skin of the chicken. Place the chicken in a large resealable plastic bag and remove all the air to allow the marinade to be in close contact with the skin. Place in the refrigerator for a minimum of 2 hours, but ideally overnight for the most flavor.

Preheat the oven to 375°F (190°C). Place the chicken, breast side up, in a roasting pan fitted with a rack. Bake, uncovered, for about 1½ hours, or until a meat thermometer inserted into the thickest portion of the thigh (not touching bone) reads 165°F (74°C) and the skin is browned and crispy. Serve with Salsa Verde Mágica (page 165).

NOTE: Both *huacatay* paste and *ají panca* paste are readily available to order online and highly recommended. However, to replace *huacatay* paste, use a mixture of 2 parts regular fresh mint, 2 parts fresh cilantro and 1 part fresh basil. Blend them together with a little olive oil to create a paste, and freeze extra in portions in an ice cube tray. You can use pasilla peppers or ancho chiles to replace the *ají panca*.

AIP COMPLIANT: Omit the *ají panca* paste and black pepper and double the amount of *huacatay* paste (or the substitute herb blend suggested in the note). Add ¾ teaspoon of ground ginger to give it a spicy kick without the nightshades. I made this dish often when I was following strict AIP.

HOME-STYLE ARROZ CON POLLO
CHICKEN WITH RICE

Puerto Rico

Arroz con pollo may sound quite plain since its name translates as "chicken with rice," but it is the very definition of hearty comfort food, not just in Puerto Rico but throughout Latin America. This is Milagros's family recipe for this classic dish. Even though rice is a grain, I think—and many Paleo diet advocates agree—that it is fine to eat white rice on occasion, as long as you don't have any negative reaction to eating it. I just couldn't leave this traditional dish out of this cookbook, but I have also included a strictly Paleo version that is quick to prepare, grain-free and low-carb (see page 91).

SERVES 6

1 (3- to 4-lb [1.4- to 1.8-kg]) whole chicken

3 tbsp (45 ml) extra-virgin olive oil, divided

2 tbsp (30 g) Sofrito (page 148; ensure that it is thawed)

1 tsp (6 g) fine Himalayan salt, divided

1 tsp (2 g) freshly ground black pepper, divided

½ tsp ground turmeric

2 cups (370 g) long-grain white rice, rinsed under running water until the water runs clear

3 cups (710 ml) Chicken Broth (page 168) or filtered water

2 tbsp (32 g) tomato paste

10 to 12 olives, pitted and sliced

NOTE: To make a nightshade-free version, use canned pure pumpkin puree in place of the tomato paste and use the AIP-compliant Sofrito (page 148). White rice is not AIP compliant, but many successfully reintroduce it to their diet.

Begin by cutting up the chicken. On a cutting board, place the chicken on its back and pull each leg away from the body, cutting through the skin toward the hip joint. Bend the leg away until the thighbone pops from its socket and use the knife to cut the leg away completely. Rotate the chicken to its side and pull each wing away from the body, using the knife to cut it off. To remove the breasts, cut downward through the rib cage and shoulder joints to separate them from the backbone. Place the breasts skin side down on the cutting board and cut them in the center to separate. Then, cut each breast in half crosswise through the bone. Place each leg skin side down and cut at the joint to separate the drumstick from the thigh. If the thighs are really huge, you can cut them in half by slicing parallel to the bone, leaving one piece with bone and one that is boneless. Remove the skin from all pieces and save it along with the backbone in a resealable plastic bag in the freezer to use for broth later (see page 168).

Now the hard work is done! In a small bowl, make an *adobo* from 1 tablespoon (15 ml) of the olive oil, the *sofrito*, ½ teaspoon of the salt, half of the pepper and the turmeric by mixing them all together to form a paste. Coat the chicken pieces with the *adobo* and allow to marinate in a covered dish in the refrigerator for at least 2 hours, up to overnight.

In a large Dutch oven or other sturdy pot with a lid, heat the remaining 2 tablespoons (30 ml) of olive oil over medium heat for 1 to 2 minutes. Place the chicken pieces in the bottom of the pot in a single layer, cover and cook for about 10 minutes. Turn each piece of chicken over, cover and cook for 10 minutes more.

Add the remaining ingredients and stir to combine. Cover and cook for 25 to 30 minutes more, until the rice is done and the chicken is cooked through. If the rice is too watery, you can leave the lid off for the last 10 minutes or so.

If you are lucky, some of the rice will caramelize at the bottom of the pot into what is lovingly called *pegao*. This burnt rice is considered a delicacy and is often fought over! Scrape it up with a wooden spoon and enjoy.

MOFONGO RELLENO DE CAMARONES
MOFONGO STUFFED WITH SHRIMP

Puerto Rico

Mofongo is one of my all-time favorite Puerto Rican dishes. It is incredible to me just how flavorful the combination of fried plantains, garlic and *chicharrónes* (cracklings) is! It can be served as a side dish (page 53), but it transforms into a hearty main dish when stuffed with shrimp cooked in a rich tomato sauce.

SERVES 4

1 batch Mofongo (page 53)

FOR THE *CAMARONES*

2 tbsp (30 ml) extra-virgin olive oil

4 tbsp (55 g) Sofrito (page 148)

2 large cloves garlic, minced

1 (15-oz [425-g]) can plain tomato sauce

1 orange or yellow bell pepper, minced

1 small onion, minced

¼ tsp fine Himalayan salt

¼ tsp freshly ground black pepper

1 lb (455 g) medium peeled and deveined shrimp

2 tbsp (2 g) minced fresh cilantro, for garnish

Cook the *mofongo* and the *camarones* simultaneously so they are both ready at the same time.

To prepare the *camarones*, in a large sauté pan, heat the olive oil over medium heat for 1 to 2 minutes, add the *sofrito* and stir for 2 to 4 minutes (longer if cooking with frozen *sofrito*), until sizzling and fragrant. Add the garlic and cook for an additional 60 seconds.

Pour in the tomato sauce, add the bell pepper, onion, salt and black pepper and bring to a simmer. Cook for 3 to 4 minutes to soften the bell pepper and onion. Add the shrimp and simmer until they are cooked through, 6 to 8 minutes.

Divide the *mofongo* into 4 portions. Shape each portion into a mound and then create an indentation in the center, forming a bowl shape (just like making mashed potato volcanoes when you were a kid!). Generously fill with the shrimp and sauce, allowing it to overflow out from the center. Garnish with the cilantro and serve immediately.

AIP COMPLIANT: Make a simple garlic-*sofrito* sauce: Omit the tomato sauce, bell pepper and black pepper and use half the amount of onion. Use an additional ¼ cup (60 ml) of extra-virgin olive oil and 2 to 4 more garlic cloves. Squeeze in the juice of 1 lime when adding the shrimp to the pan. Rather than simmer the ingredients in the tomato sauce, you will sauté everything in the olive oil. The cooking times are approximately the same.

PASTELES
GREEN BANANA TAMALES

 Puerto Rico

Puerto Rican *pasteles* are a traditional holiday dish in the tamale family, with a dough made from Paleo-friendly starchy tropical fruits, vegetables and roots. This is Milagros's family recipe, passed down for generations. Different families have different traditions for both the dough and the filling. They are labor-intensive to make but many hands make light work. It is not uncommon for families to pile together in the kitchen and make these in huge batches. They are excellent for batch cooking and store well in the freezer for six months. Unwrapping these is like opening a special present!

MAKES ABOUT 20 TO 22 *PASTELES*

FOR THE *MASA*

14 to 16 very green bananas (about 6 lbs [2.7 kg]), peeled and coarsely chopped

1½ tbsp plus 2 tsp (27 g) fine Himalayan salt, divided

3 malanga roots (about 1½ lbs [680 g]), peeled and coarsely chopped

1½ lb (680 g) calabaza squash, seeds removed, peeled and coarsely chopped (can substitute butternut or acorn)

1 cup (237 ml) Chicken Broth (page 168)

FOR THE MEAT FILLING

6 tbsp (84 g) lard, coconut oil or avocado oil

6 tbsp (85 g) Sofrito (page 148)

2 tsp (4 g) ground turmeric

1 batch Simple Shredded Chicken (page 167) or leftover Milagros's Famous Pernil al Horno (page 16), shredded

1 (2.5-oz [70-g]) jar capers, drained

4 culantro leaves, or about 12 sprigs fresh cilantro

1 tsp (2 g) dried oregano

1 tsp (6 g) fine Himalayan salt

To prepare the *masa*, cut the tips off the bananas and cut 2 to 3 slits down the length of the peel. Cut each crosswise into 3 pieces. Place in a large bowl or pot and cover with water. Dissolve 1 to 2 teaspoons (6 to 12 g) of salt in the water. Allow to soak for 20 minutes, then remove the peels. Working in batches, puree the bananas, malanga and calabaza in a food processor or blender, adding the chicken broth. In a very large mixing bowl, combine all the pureed starches with the remaining salt, thoroughly mixing the starches together. Alternatively, you can grate all the starches, using a box grater. This is the traditional method that is quite labor-intensive, though some swear by the consistency of the dough when it is made this way.

Ideally, chill the *masa* in a covered bowl in the fridge overnight. This prevents the dough from tasting bitter and also makes it easier to work with.

Also ideally, prepare the meat filling in advance so that it can also chill in the refrigerator overnight. It should not be hot when forming the *pasteles*.

To prepare the meat filling, in a large skillet, heat the fat, *sofrito* and turmeric over medium heat until sizzling and fragrant, 3 to 4 minutes. Add the meat, capers, culantro, oregano and salt and sauté until the meat is warmed through, 5 to 10 minutes. Place in an airtight container and allow to chill in the refrigerator.

Clear off your counter space and recruit help if you can. To prepare the banana leaves, spread them out and cut out the central stalk, then cut the leaves into pieces about 12 x 18 inches (30.5 x 45.5 cm). Discard any leaf sections that are ripped, which would allow the dough to leak out. Place the leaves in a stack. If using parchment paper, cut it to size and arrange in a stack.

(continued)

TO ASSEMBLE THE *PASTELES*

40 to 44 pieces thawed banana leaves, or 25 pieces plain parchment paper (optional: include a small piece of banana leaf if wrapping with paper)

22 pieces 45" (1.4 m) kitchen twine

¼ cup (60 ml) extra-virgin olive oil mixed with ½ tsp ground turmeric

½ (5.75-oz [163-g]) jar green Manzanilla olives

To assemble the *pasteles*, arrange the stack of leaves, twine, turmeric-dyed olive oil, bowl of *masa*, meat filling and olives on your counter. For each *pastele*, you will use 2 banana leaf pieces or 1 sheet of cut parchment paper (paired optionally with a small slice of banana leaf for flavor) with the long edge running left to right.

To assemble, first dip a spoon in the olive oil and spread it around the center of your wrapper. Add ½ cup (115 g) of the *masa*, 2 to 3 tablespoons (28 to 42 g) of the meat filling and 2 or 3 olives.

Fold the *pasteles* by grabbing the banana leaf edge closest to you and folding away from you, lining up the edges of the leaves. Straighten the shape of the *masa* by pressing gently with your hands below the leaf edges. Fold the edges back toward you. Then, gently press the sides to shape it into a rectangle and fold the sides toward the center, sealing the mixture inside. If necessary, repeat with a second banana leaf. Turn the wrapped *pastele* over so the folds are facing down.

If using paper, use only one piece. Follow the same process, but in the first step when lining up the edges, fold 1 inch (2.5 cm) of the edges together and crease before folding back toward you. Before folding the side to the center, fold down 2 inches (5 cm) of the ends and crease to seal the edges of the paper.

To tie the *pasteles*, take a piece of the twine and fold it in half. Place it underneath the *pastele* with the loop sticking out by several inches (several cm) and the loose ends facing toward you. Bring the loose ends over the top of the *pastele* and through the loop. Pull the loose strings to the sides of the *pastele*. As they reach the short ends, carefully flip the *pastele* over so that you can wrap them all the way around. Meet the 2 twine ends in the center, then twist them together and wrap around the center of the *pastele* one more time, then tie it in a bow.

To cook the *pasteles*, place as many that will fit in a very large pot and fill with enough water that they can float at least 2 inches (5 cm) above the bottom of the pot. Bring to a boil over high heat, then cover and lower the heat to a low boil. Cook for 30 to 35 minutes. Halfway through cooking, turn them over to ensure even cooking. Drain and cut away the twine and very carefully (do not burn your fingers on the hot water/steam) unwrap the *pasteles* and transfer directly to dinner plates (not to a serving platter—they will fall apart). Use kitchen shears to help cut away the sides of the leaves/paper, if necessary. Always check one *pastele* for doneness before opening all of them. If necessary you can rewrap and cook them for a few minutes longer.

You can freeze *pasteles* immediately after wrapping them, prior to cooking them. Milagros recommends stacking 2 to 4 together and wrapping them with aluminum foil to keep them freshest. To cook from frozen, increase the cooking time to 45 to 55 minutes. Do not thaw before boiling.

Pastele assembled and ready to wrap.

Pastele folded and ready to tie.

Pulling the strings through the loop.

Ready to flip and finish tying.

VIANDAS CON BACALAO
TROPICAL STARCHES WITH SALTED COD

 Puerto Rico

This is a very traditional Puerto Rican dish that is especially popular during Lent and around the holidays. This is the version passed down in Milagros's family. The word *viandas* describes the various starchy roots and tubers in typical Latin American cuisine. See pages 173 to 175 for more information on these starches.

SERVES 8 TO 10

1 lb (455 g) *bacalao* (salted codfish)

FOR THE *VIANDAS*

8 green bananas

1 tsp salt

½ lb (225 g) peeled yuca, cut into 2" (5-cm) cubes

½ lb (225 g) peeled malanga, cut into 2" (5-cm) cubes

½ lb (225 g) white *ñame*, cut into 2" (5-cm) cubes

FOR THE *BACALAO*

2 tbsp (30 ml) extra-virgin olive oil

2 green onions, sliced

½ large yellow onion, sliced

1 red bell pepper, sliced

2 *ajíes dulces,* or ½ small red bell pepper, minced

1 tbsp (10 g) minced garlic

FOR THE DRESSING

¼ cup (60 ml) coconut vinegar

½ cup (120 ml) extra-virgin olive oil

½ tsp fine Himalayan salt

¼ tsp freshly ground black pepper

FOR GARNISH

1 to 2 Hass avocados, peeled, pitted and cut into 6 slices each

2 to 3 plum tomatoes, cut into wedges

A day in advance, soak the *bacalao*. Place it in a bowl and cover with water, changing the water 4 to 6 times over the next 24 hours, or according to the package directions. *Bacalao* is ready when it does not taste salty. Drain the desalinated *bacalao* and shred it into small pieces, using your fingers, removing and discarding any bone pieces.

To prepare the *viandas*, cut the tips off the bananas and cut a slit down the length of the peel. Place them in a bowl and cover with water. Add the salt to the water and allow them to soak for 15 minutes to loosen the peel. Remove the peel and cut the bananas into 1-inch (2.5-cm) disks. Place the bananas, yuca, malanga and *ñame* in a large pot and cover with water. Bring to a boil over high heat and then lower the heat to a simmer. Cook for 20 minutes, or until everything is fork-tender. Drain and place in a large bowl. Set aside.

Meanwhile, prepare the *bacalao*. In a large skillet, heat the olive oil over medium heat for 1 to 2 minutes. Cook the onions, peppers and garlic for 5 to 7 minutes, until everything has softened some but is not completely wilted. Add the shredded *bacalao* and cook about 2 minutes more, just enough to warm the fish. Transfer to a bowl and set aside.

Prepare the dressing: In a bowl, combine the vinegar, olive oil, salt and black pepper.

On a large serving platter, arrange the cooked starches in a single layer. Add the *bacalao* mixture on top and pour the dressing evenly over the entire dish. Arrange the avocado slices and tomato wedges around the edges of the serving platter. For best results cover and let it chill in the refrigerator for at least 1 hour before serving as a cold salad.

AIP COMPLIANT: In the *bacalao*, omit the black pepper, bell pepper and *ajíes dulces* and add 2 tablespoons (30 g) of the AIP-compliant version of Sofrito (page 148) for flavor. In the garnish, replace the tomato with 1 medium red onion cut into thin rings.

ROPA VIEJA
SHREDDED BEEF IN TOMATO SAUCE

 Cuba

Ropa vieja literally translates as "old clothes," and the legend attached to this dish says that there was once a peasant who had no meat to feed his family, so he put his old clothes into the stew pot and they were magically transformed by his love and good intentions into this delicious dish. Others say the dish got its name because the shredded meat resembles tattered cloth. Regardless, it is a hearty, classic dish and is excellent for batch cooking.

SERVES 4 TO 6

3 tbsp (45 ml) olive oil

2 lb (905 g) flank steak, cut crosswise into 3 or 4 pieces

6 to 8 cloves garlic, minced

1 large onion, diced

1 large bell pepper (any color), seeded and diced

½ tsp fine Himalayan salt

¼ tsp freshly ground black pepper

1 (8-oz [235-g]) can plain tomato sauce

2 bay leaves

1½ tsp (3 g) dried oregano

1½ tsp (4 g) ground cumin

3 to 4 cups (710 to 946 ml) water or Chicken Broth (page 168)

1 (1-oz [28-g]) jar capers, drained

½ cup (50 g) sliced green Manzanilla olives

2 tbsp (2 g) minced fresh cilantro

In a large Dutch oven or heavy-bottomed pot, heat the olive oil over medium-high heat for 3 to 4 minutes. Brown the meat on both sides, 5 to 8 minutes. Transfer to a plate and set aside.

Lower the heat to medium and add the garlic, cooking briefly until fragrant, 15 to 20 seconds. Then, add the onion and bell pepper and cook, stirring frequently, for about 5 minutes. Add the salt, black pepper, tomato sauce, bay leaves, oregano, cumin and water or broth and bring to a boil over high heat. Return the browned meat to the pan and cover, lowering the heat to a simmer. Cook until the meat is tender and shreds easily with 2 forks, 2½ to 3 hours, stirring the pot every 30 to 45 minutes; if the sauce thickens too much, you can add extra water in ½-cup (120-ml) increments. During the last 30 minutes or so of cooking, add the capers and olives.

Once the meat is tender enough to shred, remove it from the pot and carefully shred it with 2 forks. Add the shreds back to the pot and stir in the cilantro.

Serve immediately with your favorite rice replacement (pages 116 and 118) and/or Plátanos Maduros (page 111).

NOTES: For a less hands-on cooking method, place all the ingredients, except the capers, olives and cilantro, in a slow cooker and cook on low for about 8 hours. Shred the meat, stir it together with the sauce and add the capers, olives and cilantro.

While flank steak is the traditional cut used because of the pronounced look of the cooked shreds, you may also substitute a more economical chuck roast, which usually weighs about 4 pounds (1.8 kg). Double the other ingredients and increase the cooking time to 3 to 4 hours for tender, fork-shreddable chuck. Or put it all in the slow cooker as described above.

LECHÓN ASADO
MOJO MARINATED PORK ROAST

 Cuba

The term *lechón asado* typically refers to the Cuban method for roasting a whole suckling pig, but can also mean a flavorful pork roast done right in your oven. Allowing a pork roast to marinate overnight in *mojo criollo*, which is a blend of sour orange juice and garlic, results in a moist and tender roast of which you'll certainly be asking for seconds.

SERVES 4 TO 6

1½ cups (355 ml) Mojo Criollo (page 154)

½ cup (80 g) finely diced onion

2 large onions, sliced into rings

1 (4- to 5-lb [1.8- to 2.3-kg]) bone-in pork shoulder roast

Cut slits in the skin on the top of the pork roast and pierce all sides of the roast with a knife, to help the *mojo criollo* marinade penetrate the meat. Coat the roast with the marinade and the diced onion and place in a large resealable plastic bag. Allow to marinate overnight, up to 24 hours.

Before roasting, remove the pork from the refrigerator and allow to stand at room temperature for 30 minutes. Preheat the oven to 400°F (200°C). Arrange the onion rings across the bottom of a pan that has sides a few inches (cm) tall (this is to accommodate all of the fat that renders out during roasting). Remove the pork from the bag. Place the roast, skin side up, on top of the bed of onions and roast, uncovered, for 1 hour. Then, without opening the oven, lower the temperature to 300°F (150°C) and continue to roast until a meat thermometer inserted into the thickest part of the roast (not touching the bone) reads 185°F (85°C), or 2 to 3 hours longer (40 to 45 minutes per pound [455 g] of roast). You may wish to check the roast after 1½ hours' roasting at 300°F (150°C).

The roast is done when the meat shreds easily with a fork and the fat on top is nicely crisped.

AIP COMPLIANT: Simply omit the black pepper from the *mojo criollo* marinade.

MASITAS DE PUERCO FRITAS
MOJO MARINATED AND FRIED PORK CUBES

 Cuba

At most Cuban restaurants you will see *masas de puerco* as a main dish option. Well, these are *masitas*, or "little pieces," because this version is pan-fried rather than deep-fried, and cutting the pork into small chunks makes it faster and easier to cook this dish. Marinating in *mojo criollo* gives these fried chunks of delicious pork their signature flavor. You will love the contrasting textures in this dish: crispy and caramelized on the outside, yet tender on the inside.

SERVES 6 TO 8

1 (2- to 2¼-lb [905-g to 1-kg]) pork loin roast, trimmed of fat

1 cup (235 ml) Mojo Criollo (page 154), made using only 2 tbsp (30 ml) extra-virgin olive oil

6 to 8 tbsp (84 to 112 g) lard or avocado oil for frying (using extra as needed)

1 large white onion, peeled and cut into rings, divided

Cut the trimmed loin roast into chunks no larger than 1 inch (2.5 cm) in any dimension. Place the pork chunks in an airtight container, pour in the *mojo criolo* to coat evenly and allow to marinate in the refrigerator a minimum of 4 hours, ideally overnight.

Remove the chunks from the marinade and pat them dry on paper towels. Reserve the marinade for the end of the recipe.

Preheat the oven to 275°F (140°C) to keep the pork warm as you fry it in batches.

In a medium or large skillet or Dutch oven, heat your fat of choice over medium heat until shimmering, about 5 minutes. You will need at least ½ inch (1.3 cm) of fat in the pan. (The larger the pan, the more fat you will use, but the faster you can cook the batches. It is up to you whether you prefer to use less fat or cook faster.) Add pork chunks to the hot oil without crowding the pieces and fry, turning often, until all sides are browned and crispy, 8 to 12 minutes total. Transfer with a slotted spoon to an ovenproof dish and place in the warm oven. Repeat until all the chunks are cooked.

After the last pieces of pork have been cooked, drain all but about 2 tablespoons (30 ml) of fat from the pan. Add about half of the sliced onion rings to the pan and cook briefly, about 1 minute, before adding the reserved marinade. Toss to combine and cook, stirring often, for about 5 minutes, scraping the bottom of the pan with a wooden spoon to scrape up any burnt bits. Add the remaining onion rings and continue to cook for about 5 minutes more.

Combine the cooked onions with the fried pork chunks in a serving dish and serve immediately. Pairs wonderfully with Tostones (page 115) or Plátano Maduros (page 111).

AIP COMPLIANT: Use the AIP-compliant version of Mojo Criollo (page 154).

CHAYOTES RELLENOS
CHAYOTE SQUASH STUFFED WITH MEAT

 Puerto Rico

Chayotes are delicious tropical squashes that are perfect to stuff with meat and bake like stuffed peppers. They do take quite a while to cook, though, but the hands-on time in this recipe is minimal. Make a big batch to feed a crowd. Leftovers reheat very well, too, making this recipe great for batch cooking. In addition to using the ground beef mixture provided here, you may also use any leftover Carne Molida (page 95), Picadillo (page 96) or other meat filling to stuff these.

SERVES 6 TO 8

6 large chayotes, cut in half lengthwise

1 tbsp plus 1 tsp (24 g) fine Himalayan salt

2 tbsp (30 ml) extra-virgin olive oil

2 tbsp (30 g) Sofrito (page 148)

4 medium cloves garlic, minced

1 small onion, diced finely

1 lb (455 g) ground beef

4 tbsp (64 g) tomato paste

Juice of 2 limes

2 tsp (6 g) drained capers

1 tsp (2 g) dried oregano

12 pieces "Queso" Blanco (page 170), (optional)

Place the halved chayotes in a large pot and cover with water; add the tablespoon (18 g) of the salt. Bring to a boil over high heat, then lower the heat to a low boil, cover and cook until the chayotes are fork-tender, about 45 minutes to 1 hour.

Meanwhile, in a large skillet, heat the olive oil over medium heat for 1 to 2 minutes. Add the *sofrito* and remaining teaspoon (6 g) of salt and cook for 2 to 3 minutes, until fragrant (longer if using frozen *sofrito*). Add the garlic and onion and cook for 3 to 4 minutes. Add the remaining ingredients except the "cheese" and break up the ground beef, cooking, stirring occasionally, until the meat is no longer pink, about 15 minutes. Reduce the heat to low to keep warm until the chayotes are ready.

Preheat the oven to 400°F (200°C).

Drain the chayotes and carefully scoop out and discard the tough, fibrous core from the center, leaving as much flesh as possible. Then, be very careful to scoop out the flesh while leaving the shell intact. Add the flesh to the meat mixture, increase the heat to medium and allow to simmer for 5 to 10 minutes to allow the flavors to meld.

Arrange the chayote shells on cookie sheets or in glass baking dishes and fill with the meat mixture. Bake for 10 minutes. If desired, you may top them with slices of dairy-free white cheese during the last 5 to 7 minutes of baking. Serve with your favorite side dishes.

AIP COMPLIANT: Omit the tomato paste and use canned pure pumpkin puree in its place.

SANCOCHO
TROPICAL STARCH STEW

Puerto Rico

Sancocho is a type of hearty stew popular in many countries. It is traditionally prepared on Sundays, using up leftover ingredients from the week. It is an easy one-pot meal to put together and share with loved ones. Milagros likes to use a wide variety of starchy fruits and tubers in her *sancocho* and would traditionally put corn on the cob in hers as well, which I have omitted here to keep it grain-free and Paleo. See pages 173 to 175 for more info on these tropical starches. Yuca and plantains are typically the easiest to find, and you can use another squash for the calabaza and white potatoes in place of the malanga and taro.

SERVES 6 TO 8

2 to 4 tbsp (30 to 60 ml) extra-virgin olive oil (use more if cooking raw meat)

4 tbsp (55 g) Sofrito (page 148)

1½ lb (680 g) cubed fresh meat (such as stew beef or pork or chicken breast), or about 2 cups (280 g) Simple Shredded Chicken (page 167)

1 large onion, diced

1 lb (455 g) peeled and cored yuca (frozen recommended)

1 green plantain, peeled and sliced into 1" (2.5-cm) rounds

1 ripe plantain, peeled and sliced into 1" (2.5-cm) rounds

1 small piece (½ to 1 lb [225 to 455 g]) calabaza squash, peeled and cut in 1" (2.5-cm) pieces (can substitute butternut squash or regular pumpkin)

1 to 2 malangas, peeled and cut into 1" (2.5-cm) pieces

1 small taro root, peeled and cut into 1" (2.5-cm) pieces

1 tsp (6 g) fine Himalayan salt

½ tsp freshly ground black pepper

1 tsp ground turmeric

2 to 3 quarts (1.9 to 2.8 L) Chicken Broth (page 168), divided

In a large stockpot, heat the olive oil over medium heat for 1 to 2 minutes, then add the *sofrito*. Cook, stirring constantly, until sizzling and fragrant, about 2 to 4 minutes (longer if using frozen).

If using raw meat, add it now and stir frequently to sear all sides, about 5 minutes. Add the onion and continue to sauté until it is translucent, 3 to 5 minutes more. If you are using leftover shredded meat, add it together with the onion, cooking for 3 to 5 minutes.

Use a wooden spoon to scrape up any browned bits from the bottom of the pan, if necessary, and add a few cups (235 to 475 ml) of broth to deglaze the pan. Next, add all the remaining ingredients, topping off with enough broth to cover. Note that traditionally this is not a watery soup. Bring to a boil over high heat, then cover the pot and lower the heat to a simmer. Cook for at least 30 minutes, or until all the starches are tender. Overcooking will cause the ripe plantains and calabaza to fall apart.

AIP COMPLIANT: Use the AIP-compliant version of Sofrito (page 148).

PABELLÓN CRIOLLO
SHREDDED BEEF, RIPE PLANTAINS, "BEANS" AND "RICE"

Venezuela

Pabellón criollo is considered to be the national dish of Venezuela and consists of four parts: tender shredded meat (called *carne mechada*), fried sweet plantains (called *plátanos maduros*), black beans (called *caraotas negras*) and white rice. To create a strictly Paleo version, I have devised not one but two options to replace both the white rice and the black beans. This dish is served as a hearty meal, but you can also take a small portion of each of the four components and stuff them inside an arepa (page 68) or even inside an empanada (page 50).

SERVES 4 TO 6

FOR THE *CARNE MECHADA*
2 lb (905 g) flank steak

2 onions (1 quartered, 1 diced), divided

1 bay leaf

1 fresh mint leaf, or ½ tsp dried

3 tbsp (45 ml) extra-virgin olive oil

1 red bell pepper, diced

3 large cloves garlic, minced

2 tbsp (30 ml) coconut aminos

1 tsp (5 ml) cider vinegar or lime juice

1½ tsp (9 g) fine Himalayan salt

Freshly ground black pepper

2 tbsp (2 g) chopped fresh cilantro

½ tsp ground cumin

TO SERVE
Cauliflower Rice (page 116) or White or Yellow Malanga "Rice" (page 118)

"Caraotas" Negras de Vegetales (page 127) or "Caraotas" Negras de Yuca (page 129)

2 or 3 yellow plantains, cooked according to the directions for Plátanos Maduros on page 111

To prepare the *carne mechada*, cut the flank steak crosswise into 2 or 3 pieces and place in a large pot. Add the quartered onion, bay leaf and mint and cover everything with water. Bring to a boil over high heat, then cover and lower the heat to a moderate simmer. Cook until the steak is falling-apart tender, 2½ to 3 hours. During the last half hour or so of cooking, you can work on preparing the rice, beanless *caraotas* and plantains.

When the meat is cooked, remove the steak and shred with 2 forks. Strain the broth and reserve for another use, discarding the cooked onion and leaves.

In a large skillet, heat the olive oil over medium heat for 2 to 3 minutes. Add the diced onion and red pepper and cook for 6 to 8 minutes. Add all the remaining *carne mechada* ingredients and mix well, then stir in the shredded beef. Let it all simmer together for about 5 minutes to let the flavors meld.

When plating the *pabellón criollo*, you can divide the plate into 4 equal quarters and fill one with *carne mechada*, one with rice, one with the beanless *caraotas* and one with fried plantain slices. Alternatively, you can arrange the 4 components in parallel lines across the plate.

> **AIP COMPLIANT:** In the *carne mechada*, omit the red bell pepper, black pepper and cumin.

¡COMIDA DE FIESTA!

PARTY FOOD!

There is nothing that says "It's time to party!" like a plate of crispy and delicious fried food. Even though the fried dishes in this chapter are pan-fried, using healthy fats, they still should not make up the bulk of your healthy Paleo diet. However, they are so much fun that you will forget you are even eating a restricted diet! It is recipes like these that help make the Paleo diet sustainable in the long term. If you aren't having fun and don't feel that you can treat yourself to something special, you can quickly get bored. Deep-frying in healthy Paleo cooking fats can get expensive quickly. That's why I've adapted these recipes for easy pan-frying (though that sometimes results in less-than-perfect shapes). Your taste buds won't notice one bit, I promise!

Also, please feel free to experiment with the fillings. I have provided you with traditional recipes, but there is no reason you can't swap out the type of meat filling inside of these fritters. You can even use leftover shredded meats from the "Platos de la Familia" chapter in many of these dishes. Have fun with it!

Pupusas con Chicharrón o "Queso", recipe on page 63.

EMPANADAS AL HORNO
BAKED MEAT TURNOVERS

Argentina

If you are looking for something festive and fun but not fried, these Argentinean-style empanadas are just the thing you need! When forming the empanadas, the traditional look is a folded decorative edge called *repulgo*, which takes extra care to shape with this gluten-free dough. The filling provided is typical for Argentina; however, you can feel free to test other filling recipes from this book.

MAKES 8 EMPANADAS

FOR THE FILLING

3 tbsp (45 ml) extra-virgin olive oil

1½ tsp (5 g) minced garlic (about 2 large cloves)

1 large onion, diced

1 small red bell pepper, diced

1 tsp (6 g) fine Himalayan salt

1 tsp (2 g) freshly ground black pepper

½ tsp paprika

¼ to ½ tsp red pepper flakes or cayenne pepper

1 tsp (3 g) ground cumin

1 tsp (2 g) dried oregano

½ lb (225 g) ground beef

FOR THE DOUGH

1½ cups (180 g) sifted cassava flour

¼ cup (32 g) tapioca starch

1 tsp (6 g) fine Himalayan salt

¼ cup (56 g) palm shortening or lard

2 tbsp (30 g) canned pure pumpkin puree, or 1 large egg, beaten

¾ cup (175 ml) coconut milk

First, prepare the filling. This gives it a chance to cool before you form the empanadas. Because these bake for quite a while, you do not want to overcook the beef in the skillet.

In a large skillet, heat the olive oil over medium heat for 1 to 2 minutes. Add the garlic and cook until fragrant, about 1 minute. Add the onion and cook until it has begun to soften, about 5 minutes. Add the bell pepper, salt, black pepper, paprika, red pepper or cayenne, cumin and oregano and cook for another 3 to 4 minutes. Add the ground beef and stir to break it up, cooking for 5 to 7 minutes more, or until it is just cooked through. Strain the meat mixture with a slotted spoon into a bowl, cover and place in the refrigerator to chill.

Preheat the oven to 375°F (190°C).

Next, prepare the empanada dough: In a mixing bowl, combine the cassava flour, tapioca starch and salt and use a fork to cut the shortening into the flour. If using pumpkin instead of egg, cut it into the flour with the fat. Stir in the coconut milk (and egg, if using) until a dough forms. Use your hands to work the dough into a ball, then divide it into 8 portions.

(continued)

TO ASSEMBLE THE EMPANADAS

1 large egg, hard-boiled and chopped coarsely

⅓ cup (34 g) chopped green Manzanilla olives

1 large egg beaten with 1 tbsp (15 ml) water, for the glaze (can substitute olive oil)

To assemble the empanadas, take each portion and roll it into a ball between your hands. Place it between 2 pieces of parchment paper. Place a plate on top of the ball and use even pressure to press down to flatten the ball into a disk, then use a rolling pin to flatten it to about 5 inches (12.5 cm) across. Fill with about 1 tablespoon (15 g) of the meat mixture plus about 1 teaspoon (5 g) each of the chopped egg and olives. Use the parchment paper to assist in folding the empanada. For the traditional Argentinean look, close the empanada using the decorative *repulgo* folds: Make a triangular pleat at one end and continue to fold more triangular pleats all the way across the edge until it is sealed.

Arrange the empanadas on a baking sheet and brush the tops with the egg wash (or olive oil). Bake them for about 35 minutes, or until the tops are lightly golden and crisp. Let cool briefly before serving.

AIP COMPLIANT: Use the AIP-compliant version of Carne Molida (page 95) in place of the filling, cooked according to AIP instructions, or another AIP meat of choice. Instead of brushing the tops with egg wash, simply brush with extra-virgin olive oil.

MOFONGO
MASHED GREEN PLANTAINS AND FRIED PORK BELLY

 Puerto Rico

Your taste buds won't believe just how flavorful this simple green plantain dish is. It makes a wonderful appetizer dish to share or can work wonderfully as a starchy side to pair with your favorite protein. You can also turn it into a full-blown meal by stuffing it with meat (see Mofongo Relleno de Camarones, page 30). Hands down, this is my favorite way to cook green plantain and one of the dishes that helped me stay motivated when I was strictly AIP.

SERVES 4 TO 6

4 green plantains, peeled and sliced

About ¼ cup (56 g) fat of choice for frying (lard, bacon fat or avocado oil recommended)

4 medium cloves garlic, minced

¾ to 1 cup (98 to 130 g) crushed Chicharrónes (page 75), pork rinds or crispy bacon, coarsely chopped

1 to 3 tsp (6 to 18 g) fine Himalayan salt

1 tsp (2 g) dried oregano (optional)

2 to 4 tbsp (30 to 60 ml) extra-virgin olive oil

Slice off the tips of the plantain with a knife, then cut 1 or 2 slits in the skin down the length of the plantain. If the peel does not lift off easily, you can soak the plantains in a bowl with water and about 1 teaspoon (6 g) of salt for 10 to 15 minutes to loosen the skin.

Slice the peeled plantain crosswise into disks ½ to ¾ inch (1.3 to 2 cm) wide. Don't cut them too thickly or they won't cook in the center.

In a large skillet, heat your fat of choice over medium heat until shimmering, 3 to 5 minutes. Carefully add the disks to the heated fat and cook for 3 to 4 minutes per side, or until they have turned a darker, more golden color. Do not allow to brown. You should be able to easily pierce them with a fork. Add extra cooking fat to the pan as needed, because green plantains can soak up a lot of it.

While the plantains are frying, place the garlic, crushed *chicharrónes*, salt and optional oregano in a mixing bowl and stir to combine. Taste and adjust salt as desired.

Add the fried plantains and any fat from the skillet to the mixing bowl and use a potato masher or a sturdy fork to mash the plantains and mix them together with the garlic and pork. Add the olive oil 1 tablespoon (15 ml) at a time and mix until you are able to form the *mofongo* into balls that hold their shape. If it crumbles, it is too dry and needs more oil.

If serving as an appetizer, form the *mofongo* into balls about the size of a golf ball. If serving as a side dish, divide into 4 to 6 equal portions and use a small ramekin or cup to form them into a mound shape and then release the shaped *mofongo* onto the serving plate.

Best served immediately.

PASTELILLOS
FRIED MEAT TURNOVERS

 Puerto Rico

Pastelillos are the first Puerto Rican meal I ever cooked, and from then on I was totally hooked on the cuisine. They are a type of fried empanada with a wide crispy edge and are dangerously hard to stop eating once you have had a taste. They are a typical roadside food in Puerto Rico that serves as an easy option for a portable lunch.

MAKES 8 PASTELILLOS

½ cup (85 g) Carne Molida (page 95) or meat filling of choice

1½ cups (180 g) sifted cassava flour

¼ cup (32 g) tapioca starch

1 tsp (6 g) fine Himalayan salt

¼ cup (56 g) palm shortening or lard

2 tbsp (30 g) canned pure pumpkin puree, or 1 large egg, beaten

¾ cup (175 ml) coconut milk

About ¼ cup (60 ml) avocado oil for frying, using extra as needed

Prepare and chill the *carne molida* or other meat filling of choice in advance so that it is chilled when you are assembling the *pastelillos*.

In a mixing bowl, combine the cassava flour, tapioca starch and salt and use a fork to cut the shortening into the flour. If using pumpkin instead of egg, cut it into the flour with the fat. Stir in the coconut milk (and egg, if using) until a dough forms. Use your hands to work the dough into a ball, then divide it into 8 portions.

Take each portion and roll it into a ball between your hands. Place it between 2 pieces of parchment paper. Place a plate on top of the ball and use even pressure to press down to flatten the ball into a disk, then use a rolling pin to flatten it to 5 to 6 inches (12.5 to 15 cm) across. Fill with about 1 tablespoon (15 g) of the meat filling. Use the parchment paper to assist in folding the dough over to seal. Line up the edges and then press them closed, using the tines of a fork for a crimped look. The edge should be about 1 inch (2.5 cm) wide.

In a small or medium skillet, heat the oil for 4 to 5 minutes, then carefully add the *pastelillos*, working in batches if necessary. Fry them for 4 to 5 minutes per side, or until crispy and golden all over. Drain on a paper towel–lined plate. Serve immediately.

> **AIP COMPLIANT:** Use the AIP-compliant version of Carne Molida (page 95) and canned pure pumpkin puree instead of egg in the dough.

BACALAÍTOS
SALTED COD FRITTERS

 Puerto Rico

Bacalaítos are a wonderful treat for any Puerto Rican. You should see the look of excitement on the faces of both Milagros and my husband when you mention these! This batter is so authentic tasting that it is hard to believe it's not full of gluten. Milagros told me that growing up in the mountainous region of Arecibo in Puerto Rico, she rarely ate seafood. The one exception was *bacalao*, which is salt-preserved cod. Fresh poached cod will work and is also delicious, but the texture is less dense.

MAKES 12 TO 14 SMALL FRITTERS; SERVES 4 TO 6

8 oz (225 g) *bacalao* or poached fresh cod

2 tbsp (14 g) sifted coconut flour

1 cup (120 g) sifted cassava flour

½ tsp fine Himalayan salt

½ tsp freshly ground black pepper

1 tbsp (10 g) minced garlic

1 tbsp (1 g) minced culantro or cilantro

1½ cups (355 g) sparkling water

About ¼ cup (56 g) fat of choice for frying (lard, coconut oil or avocado oil)

A day in advance, soak the *bacalao*. Place it in a bowl and cover with water, changing the water 4 to 6 times over the next 24 hours, or according to the package directions. *Bacalao* is ready when it does not taste salty. Drain the desalinated *bacalao* and shred it into small pieces using your fingers, removing and discarding any bone fragments.

In a mixing bowl, combine the coconut flour, cassava flour, salt, pepper, garlic and culantro and stir well. Pour in the sparkling water and stir until a batter forms. Stir in the *bacalao* shreds.

In a small or medium skillet, heat your fat of choice. (Using a smaller pan means you use less fat, but it takes longer to cook all the fritters.)

Traditionally, *bacalaítos* are quite large, but due to the blend of gluten-free flours these are easier to cook if you make them smaller, 3 to 4 inches (7.5 to 10 cm) in diameter. Pour portions of the batter into your heated fat and cook for 2 to 3 minutes per side, until golden brown and crispy. Drain on a paper towel–lined plate. Cook the fritters in batches until all the batter is used up.

Serve immediately, pairing with a dipping sauce from the "Los Esenciales" chapter, if desired.

NOTE: If using fresh cod, cook it in boiling water until the flesh is tender and flaky, about 5 to 8 minutes, then shred.

AIP COMPLIANT: Omit the black pepper.

PANDEBONO

"CHEESE" BUNS

Colombia

Pandebono is a type of cheese bread that can be served for breakfast or a snack. These rolls are naturally gluten-free and are made with tapioca starch and sometimes blended with a type of corn flour called *masarepa* (the same flour traditionally used to make arepas) and generous amounts of cheese. I had to develop a dairy-free cheese that could withstand baking to sucessfully make these buns. This is one of the best Paleo bread replacements I have ever created (and that is saying a lot!).

MAKES 4 BUNS

1 cup (128 g) tapioca starch

1½ tbsp (11 g) sifted coconut flour

½ tsp cream of tartar

¼ tsp baking soda

½ tsp fine Himalayan salt

1 large egg, or 4 tbsp (60 g) canned pure pumpkin puree

½ batch "Queso" Blanco (page 170)

Preheat the oven to 400°F (200°C).

In a food processor, combine all the ingredients and pulse several times until everything just comes together to form a lumpy dough. Overprocessing will make the dough extremely sticky and harder to work with. Scrape the dough out with a spatula.

Due to the nature of the dairy-free cheese, the batter is sticky no matter what. You can lightly grease your hands and spatula to help prevent sticking. You can also sprinkle a small amount of tapioca starch on the outside of the buns to assist in shaping them.

Divide into 4 equal portions, handling the dough very gently and not pressing too hard on it. Very carefully form the portions into ball shapes, but do not worry if the dough is too sticky to smooth over—it will still bake up smoothly. Place the buns on a light-colored baking sheet and bake for 16 to 18 minutes, or until the tops are lightly golden. Serve immediately because tapioca starch baked goods harden as they cool.

AIP COMPLIANT: Use canned pure pumpkin puree instead of egg and bake for 15 minutes.

ALCAPURRIAS
GREEN BANANA FRITTERS

Puerto Rico

I remember visiting Puerto Rico about six months after going Paleo and being so excited that I could purchase *alcapurrias* from street vendors without any worry of gluten contamination. I remember how luxurious it felt to be able to eat a meat-stuffed fritter that was naturally Paleo. The blend of green banana and malanga yields a dough that is soft in the middle and crisp on the outside.

MAKES 16 TO 18 FRITTERS; SERVES 8 TO 10 PEOPLE

1¼ cups (216 g) Carne Molida (page 95) for authenticity, or other meat filling of your choosing

4 very green bananas, peeled

4 to 5 tsp (24 to 30 g) fine Himalayan salt, divided

2 lb (905 g) malanga or taro, peeled

1 tbsp (15 ml) extra-virgin olive oil, plus more for parchment paper

3 tbsp (45 ml) freshly squeezed lime juice

1 tbsp (10 g) minced garlic

1½ tsp (3 g) freshly ground black pepper

1 tbsp (7 g) ground turmeric

¼ to ⅓ cup (56 to 75 g) fat for frying (lard or avocado oil recommended)

Prepare and chill the *carne molida* or other meat filling of choice in advance so that it is chilled when you are assembling the *alcapurrias*.

Cut the tips off the bananas and cut 2 to 3 slits in the peel down the length of each, then slice each banana into 3 pieces. Place the pieces in a bowl with sufficient water to cover and stir in 2 teaspoons (12 g) of salt. Soak for 15 minutes to ensure the bananas are easy to peel.

After soaking, remove the peels by lifting them away with your fingers or cutting away with a knife. Place the pieces in a food processor (recommended) or blender.

Peel the malanga, chop roughly and add to the food processor. Add all the remaining ingredients, except the meat filling and the fat, and blend until a smooth dough forms, scraping down the sides 2 to 3 times. Place the dough in a mixing bowl and allow it to rest for 15 minutes (this is important and allows the dough to firm up to the correct texture).

Use a piece of parchment paper to form the *alcapurrias*: Grease an area 6 to 8 inches (15 to 20.5 cm) across with olive oil and rub a bit into your hands as well. Measure ¼ cup (60 g) of dough into the greased area and smooth it into a flat disk with the back of a spoon. Place about 1 tablespoon (15 g) of the meat filling in the center. Fold the paper together so that the dough folds over the filling. Use your (oiled) hands to form the dough into a cylinder shape, ensuring that the meat is completely covered with dough.

In a small or medium skillet, heat your fat of choice over medium heat for about 5 minutes, until shimmering. Carefully slip the *alcapurrias* into the hot oil, using a spoon to help push them off the paper if necessary. Fry in batches, cooking for 2 to 3 minutes on each side, until they are browned and crispy. Drain on a paper towel–lined plate and serve hot. Enjoy alone or dipped in Ajilimójili Sauce (page 151).

AIP COMPLIANT: Omit the black pepper.

PUPUSAS CON CHICHARRÓN O "QUESO"
STUFFED "CORN" TORTILLAS

El Salvador

Pupusas are a beloved dish in El Salvador. The dough is traditionally made from *masa harina* (nixtamalized corn, which tortillas are also made from), which was tough to replace but I think this blend of flours works very well. This type of seasoned pork filling is called *chicharrón*, but it is not to be confused with fried pork belly (page 75)—yes, different countries use the same word to mean different things! You can also fill them with "Queso" Amarillo (page 169), or even a blend of a little meat and a little "cheese." Have fun with it!

MAKES 8 PUPUSAS

FOR THE *CHICHARRÓN* FILLING

1 lb (455 g) ground pork

¾ tsp (5 g) fine Himalayan salt

½ tsp (1 g) freshly ground black pepper

½ medium tomato, diced

½ medium onion, diced

2 tsp (4 g) dried oregano

FOR THE DOUGH

1 cup (112 g) sifted coconut flour

1 cup (128 g) tapioca starch

½ tsp fine Himalayan salt

1½ cups (355 ml) filtered water

Olive oil, for forming the dough

8 slices "Queso" Amarillo (page 169), optional

2 tbsp (28 g) fat of choice for frying (lard, ghee, coconut oil or avocado oil), plus extra as needed

Curtido (page 162), for garnish

First, prepare the filling. Heat a large skillet over medium heat for 1 to 2 minutes. Add the ground pork and cook, stirring occasionally, for about 5 minutes. Add the remaining filling ingredients to the pan and cook for an additional 5 to 10 minutes, or until the pork is cooked through. Remove from the heat and allow to cool while you prepare the dough.

To prepare the dough, it is important to measure coconut flour precisely. I prefer measuring for baked goods by weight rather than volume since it is more accurate. I use a fine-mesh strainer to sift my flours, then scoop with my measuring cups and level with a knife.

In a large mixing bowl, combine the flours and salt and stir well. Add the water and use a spoon to stir and form a dough. Continue to work the dough using your hands, then allow the dough to rest for several minutes to soak up the water.

Rub a little olive oil into your hands to make it easier to work with the dough. Divide the dough into 8 portions. Roll a portion into a ball between your palms, then press your thumb in the middle a few times to form a pocket. Add about 2 tablespoons (30 g) of the filling, a slice of "Queso," or a mixture of both, and press the opening closed. Gently flatten the ball into a disk shape. Repeat with the remaining dough.

In a medium skillet, heat your fat of choice over medium heat for 2 to 3 minutes. Cook the *pupusas* in batches so you don't overcrowd the pan. Cook them for 3 to 4 minutes on each side, or until browned and crispy. Drain on a paper towel–lined plate.

Serve with generous amounts of *curtido*. This recipe works well to make a double or triple batch of *pupusas* and freeze for later. To reheat from frozen, cook in a skillet for 5 to 10 minutes, or until warmed through.

AIP COMPLIANT: Omit the tomato from the *chicharrón* filling and replace with ¼ cup (60 g) of canned pure pumpkin puree.

NOTE: The *pupusas* will hold their shape more easily if the meat filling is chilled. You can place the meat in the freezer to chill it quickly, or simply make the meat filling in advance and refrigerate it.

ABORRAJADOS DE PLÁTANO
"CHEESE"-STUFFED FRIED RIPE PLANTAINS

Colombia

Aborrajados are cheese-stuffed ripe plantains that are battered and fried. This special dairy-free white cheese I developed for this recipe is out of this world good and reminds me a little *too* much of a stretchy white cheese like mozzarella. The best part? It's nut-free and suitable for the AIP, too! You can also add a small slice of guava paste to turn these into a dessert. Or, if you aren't a fan of cheese, you can stuff these only with guava paste. Versatility is awesome!

SERVES 2 TO 4

2 large ripe plantains (yellow with some black)

About ¼ cup (56 g) fat of choice for frying (coconut oil works well)

2 large eggs, beaten

2 tbsp (30 ml) coconut milk

¼ cup (30 g) cassava flour

1 tbsp (15 g) coconut sugar or grated *panela*

8 slices "Queso" Blanco (page 170)

8 slices guava paste (optional)

Slice the tips off the plantains with a knife, then cut a slit in the skin down the length of the plantain. Lift off the peel with your fingers. Cut each plantain crosswise into 8 equal pieces.

In a medium skillet, heat your fat of choice over medium heat until shimmering, 3 to 5 minutes. Carefully add the plantain chunks to the heated fat (they should sizzle when dropped in), cooking on each side for 3 to 5 minutes, or until they have turned a nice golden brown and have partially caramelized. Be careful not to burn.

Meanwhile, prepare the batter by combining the eggs, coconut milk, cassava flour and sugar in a bowl.

Transfer the fried plantains to a paper towel–lined plate, reserving the frying oil in the pan. Place the plantain pieces between 2 sheets of parchment paper and flatten. You can use a small plate and press down with even force to do this easily and without burning your hands. Place a slice of "cheese" and/or a slice of guava paste in the center of the flattened plantain. Place a second flattened plantain on top and press the edges together to seal the filling inside.

Dip the stuffed plantain in the batter, allowing the excess to drip away, then fry for 1 to 3 minutes per side, or until golden brown and lightly crisp. Drain on a paper towel–lined plate and serve immediately.

> **AIP COMPLIANT:** Omit the eggs from the batter and add an extra ¼ cup (60 ml) of coconut milk plus 6 tablespoons (90 ml) of water to make a smooth batter and fry quickly to prevent burning.

AREPAS COLOMBIANAS
SAVORY "CORN" PANCAKES

Colombia

Arepas in Colombia are similar to those made in Venezuela, but you will most typically see them made as flat pancakes with meats and cheeses placed directly on top, as opposed to the thicker patties that are cut open and stuffed in Venezuela. This dough is simpler than the Venezuelan dough in this cookbook since it does not require the mashed potato.

MAKES 4 AREPAS

1 cup (128 g) arrowroot starch

½ cup (56 g) sifted coconut flour

½ tsp cream of tartar

¼ tsp baking soda

½ tsp fine Himalayan salt

2 tbsp (28 g) palm shortening or lard

2 tbsp (30 g) canned pure pumpkin puree, or 1 large egg, beaten

1 to 2 tbsp (15 to 30 ml) extra-virgin olive oil or lard for frying

Pollo Desmechado (page 98), dairy-free cheese (page 169 or 170), *carne mechada* (page 47), Reina Pepiada (page 84) or any of your favorite meats from this cookbook (optional), for serving

In a mixing bowl, combine the arrowroot starch, coconut flour, cream of tartar, baking soda and salt. Use a fork to cut the shortening into the flour mixture. Add the pumpkin puree (or egg) and ½ cup plus 1 tablespoon (135 ml) of water. Use your hands to work into a dough.

Divide the dough into 4 portions. Roll each into a ball and then flatten into a disk no more than ½ inch (1.3 cm) thick.

Preheat the oven to 375°F (190°C).

In a large skillet, heat the fat in over medium heat for 2 to 3 minutes. Fry the arepas for 2 to 3 minutes per side until lightly golden, but not too much. Place on a baking sheet and brush with a little extra fat if any areas seem dry.

Bake for 13 to 15 minutes, or until golden brown.

To serve, top with *pollo desmechado*. You can also make an *arepa con queso* by placing a large slice of dairy-free cheese on top. Bake it with the "Queso" Blanco (page 170) on top for about 5 minutes, or the "Queso" Amarillo (page 169) for 1 to 2 minutes. You can also top it with traditional Venezuelan fillings *carne mechada* or *reina pepiada* or another meat of your choosing.

AIP COMPLIANT: Use canned pure pumpkin puree instead of the egg.

AREPAS RELLENAS
SAVORY STUFFED "CORN" PANCAKES

Venezuela

The secret to getting Paleo arepas that are crispy on the outside and breadlike on the inside (rather than chewy) is to use mashed potato or mashed yuca in the dough. The result is incredible texture-wise and it's hard to believe you are eating grain-free bread! It is well worth the extra step to include the mashed tuber. Potato gives the softest texture, but is a nightshade, so if you are avoiding them, use yuca instead.

MAKES 4 AREPAS

1 cup (128 g) arrowroot starch

½ cup (56 g) sifted coconut flour

½ tsp cream of tartar

¼ tsp baking soda

½ tsp fine Himalayan salt

2 tbsp (28 g) palm shortening or lard

2 tbsp (30 g) canned pure pumpkin puree, or 1 large egg, beaten

½ cup (113 g) boiled and mashed potatoes or yuca (from 4 to 5 oz [115 to 140 g] peeled root, boiled for 20 minutes)

2 tbsp (30 ml) extra-virgin olive oil

2 cups (460 g) hot *carne mechada* (page 47) or chilled Reina Pepiada (page 84)

In a mixing bowl, combine the arrowroot starch, coconut flour, cream of tartar, baking soda and salt. Use a fork to cut the shortening into the flour mixture. Add the pumpkin puree (or egg), mashed potatoes and ½ cup (120 ml) of water. Use your hands to work into a dough.

Divide the dough into 4 portions. Roll each into a ball and then flatten into a disk 4 to 5 inches (10 to 12.5 cm) in diameter and about ½ inch (1.3 cm) thick in the middle. Leave the disks somewhat convex so that the edges taper down to ¼ inch (6 mm) thick.

Preheat the oven to 375°F (190°C).

In a large skillet, heat the olive oil over medium heat for 2 to 3 minutes. Fry the arepas for 2 to 3 minutes per side until lightly browned, but not too much. Place on a baking sheet and brush with a little extra oil.

Bake for 15 to 18 minutes, or until golden brown. Let rest for about 5 minutes before slicing open. Cut about two-thirds of the way through each arepa. Stuff with about ½ cup (115 g) of *carne mechada* or *reina pepiada*.

AIP COMPLIANT: Use mashed yuca instead of potato and canned pure pumpkin puree instead of egg.

CARIMAÑOLAS
MEAT STUFFED YUCA FRITTERS

Colombia

Carimañolas are traditional fare in several countries in Latin America, but this recipe is Colombian style. They are made with a simple dough of boiled and mashed yuca root that is stuffed with flavorful ground beef and then fried. The texture of fried yuca dough really is incredible without any flours needing to be added to the mashed root. Note that you need to make the filling ahead to give it time to chill before stuffing into the dough. If it is hot, the dough will fall apart.

MAKES 8 CARIMAÑOLAS

FOR THE FILLING

2 tbsp (30 ml) olive oil or lard

½ lb (225 g) ground beef or pork

½ small onion, diced (about 1 cup [160 g])

2 large cloves garlic, minced

1 tsp (2 g) dried oregano

Juice of ½ lime

2 small tomatoes, diced, with juices

1 red, orange or yellow bell pepper, seeded and diced

¼ cup (4 g) chopped fresh cilantro

FOR THE DOUGH

1½ lb (680 g) peeled yuca, cut into pieces about 3" (7.5 cm) long

1½ tsp (9 g) fine Himalayan salt

About ¼ cup (56 g) fat of choice for frying (avocado oil or lard work well)

NOTE: It is much easier and economical to work with frozen yuca. Check at your local Latin American or Asian market.

AIP COMPLIANT: Omit the tomatoes and peppers from the filling and replace with 4 tablespoons (60 g) of canned pure pumpkin puree and ½ cup (65 g) of diced carrot.

Prepare the filling. Do this step in advance to allow it to chill before frying.

In a large skillet, heat the fat over medium heat for 1 to 2 minutes. Add the ground meat and remaining filling ingredients, except the cilantro, and stir to combine well. Break up the meat with a wooden spoon.

Cook until the meat is cooked through, 10 to 15 minutes. Transfer to a container with a lid and stir in the cilantro. Place in the refrigerator to chill; alternatively, to expedite chilling, use a freezer-safe container and place in the freezer while the yuca is cooking.

To prepare the dough, place the yuca in a medium pot of water and bring it to a boil over high heat, then lower the heat slightly to a simmer. Cook for 20 to 25 minutes, until the yuca is fork-tender.

Drain the yuca and remove the stringy, fibrous core from each piece, if necessary (it is sometimes already removed from frozen yuca). It can easily be lifted out with a fork. Place the yuca in a large bowl and mash vigorously with a potato masher until completely smooth. Add the salt. Allow to cool several minutes.

Divide the yuca dough into 8 equal portions, roughly ¼ cup (60 g) in size. Lay out a sheet of parchment paper to work on. Roll a piece into a ball in your hands, then flatten into a disk about 4 inches (10 cm) in diameter. If the dough is sticky, dip your fingers in a bowl of water to prevent sticking.

Place about 4 tablespoons (60 g) of filling in the center of the disk and lift the sides to seal the dough around the filling. Smooth out any seams by rubbing gently with water. Repeat until you have formed all 8 *carimañolas*.

To save on the amount of fat used, fry the *carimañolas* in batches in a small, heavy-bottomed pot with high sides: Heat about ¾ inch (2 cm) of fat in your pot until shimmering, then carefully add the *carimañolas*. Fry them for about 5 minutes per side, until crispy and lightly golden in color. Drain on a paper towel–lined plate and serve immediately! Serve with Ají Picante (page 161).

PATACÓN MARACUCHO
FRIED PLANTAIN SANDWICH

Venezuela

This traditional Venezuelan sandwich is naturally Paleo because it utilizes two large slices of fried plantain instead of bread. How fun is that? These are best served with the plantains fresh out of the skillet. Use your imagination with the filling, combining sauces from the final chapter, "Los Esenciales," and meats from anywhere in the book.

MAKES 2 SANDWICHES

1 green plantain, peeled and cut in half crosswise, then cut in half lengthwise

¼ cup (56 g) lard, avocado oil or coconut oil

About 1 cup (230 g) filling of choice: *carne mechada* (page 47), Reina Pepiada (page 84], Pollo Desmechado (page 95), sliced Churrasco (page 105)

Sauce(s) of choice: Salsa de Ajo (page 157), Salsa Verde Mágica (page 165), Chimichurri (page 158), Ají Picante (page 161)

Shredded lettuce and/or tomato slices (optional)

Prepare the plantain "bread": Slice the tips off the plantain with a knife, then cut 1 or 2 slits in the skin down the length of the plantain. If the peel does not lift off easily at this point, you can soak the plantain in a bowl with water and about 1 teaspoon (6 g) of salt for 10 to 15 minutes to loosen the skin.

In a large skillet, heat your fat of choice over medium heat until shimmering, 3 to 5 minutes. Carefully add the plantain pieces to the heated fat, cooking on each side for 3 to 5 minutes, or until they have turned a darker, more golden color. Do not allow to brown. Drain on a paper towel-lined plate.

Use a large plate, cutting board or baking sheet to flatten the plantains: Place the plantain pieces between 2 pieces of parchment paper to prevent sticking. Press firmly and evenly. Take care not to break up the pieces once they are flat.

Working in batches, return the flattened plantains to the hot fat and fry for an additional 3 to 5 minutes per side, until browned and crispy.

Drain on a paper towel–lined plate.

Serve fresh with the filling and sauce of your choice. Some suggested pairings: *carne mechada* with *salsa verde mágica*; sliced *churrasco* steak with *chimichurri*; *reina pepiada* with tomato slices; *pollo desmechado* with *ají picante*.

AIP COMPLIANT: Omit the tomato slices and just ensure that you choose AIP-compliant sauces and fillings, which is easy to do!

CHICHARRÓNES
FRIED PORK BELLY

Colombia

In most of Latin America, *chicharrónes* are crispy pieces of pork belly and/or skin that have been slowly fried in their own rendered fat (in El Salvador, though, it can refer to a pork filling for *pupusas*; see page 63). The belly is the cut of meat from which bacon is made, which helps explain why *chicharrónes* are so absolutely delicious. The only downside about *chicharrónes* is that it does take patience to get to enjoy these crunchy treats, but it is well worth the wait to cook them up fresh at home! In Colombia these are often served as part of a full meal known as *bandeja paisa*: with rice, beans, shredded meat, sausage, eggs, plantains, avocado and small arepas.

SERVES 4

1½ lb (680 g) fresh pork belly, cut into strips 4" to 6" (10 to 15 cm) long and 1" (2.5 cm) wide

1 tsp (5 g) baking soda

Salt and freshly ground black pepper

2 limes, cut into wedges

The day before cooking, coat the belly with the baking soda and place it in a covered dish in the refrigerator. This helps improve the rate of browning as the belly fries, yielding a crispy yet tender final product.

Rinse off the baking soda and pat the meat dry. Make crosswise cuts in the meaty side of each strip about every 2 inches (5 cm), being careful not to cut through the fatty layer just below the skin. The cuts allow for even cooking.

In a large pot, combine 2 cups (475 ml) of water and the belly strips and bring to a boil over high heat, then lower the heat to a simmer and cover. Cook for about 30 minutes. Very carefully (the fat that is rendering out will be splattering) remove the lid and turn each piece of pork belly over. Continue to cook until all of the water has evaporated, about 1 hour more.

Increase the heat to medium and allow the strips to fry in the rendered fat until they are golden brown on all sides, 15 to 20 minutes more.

Remove the crispy pieces from the pan and drain on paper towels. Season with salt and pepper to taste. Serve with lime wedges.

AIP COMPLIANT: Omit the black pepper.

MINI PAPAS RELLENAS
MINI STUFFED POTATO BALLS

 *Cuba & Puerto Rico*

Papas rellenas are a popular lunch-on-the-go option in both Cuba and Puerto Rico. The dough is made from mashed potatoes and stuffed with seasoned ground beef. You can use your choice of filling here to suit your mood. Note that *papas rellenas* are traditionally made to be much larger than this and are cooked in a deep fryer. Since these are pan-fried, it is much easier to make a mini version so that they cook evenly.

SERVES 2 TO 4

1 to 1½ lb (455 to 680 g) baking potatoes, peeled and quartered

2 tbsp (28 g) lard or palm shortening

½ tsp fine Himalayan salt

½ tsp freshly ground black pepper

2 to 3 tbsp (16 to 24 g) tapioca starch

1 cup (170 g) chilled ground meat filling of choice: Picadillo (page 96) or Carne Molida (page 95)

About ¼ cup (56 g) lard, coconut oil or avocado oil for frying

Place the quartered potatoes in a large pot with a lid and cover with water. Bring to a boil over high heat, then lower the heat to a gentle boil and cover. Cook until the potatoes are tender, 15 to 20 minutes.

Drain the potatoes and place in a mixing bowl. Use a potato masher or a fork to mash the potatoes until smooth. Add the lard, salt, pepper and tapioca starch and mix to combine evenly into a dough. You should be able to form balls without the dough cracking. Allow the dough to cool enough to handle (you can place it in the fridge for a few minutes, if necessary).

Take 2 tablespoons (28 g) of the dough and roll it into a ball between your hands. Flatten the ball and curve your palm to make a bowl shape. Add a heaping ½ tablespoon (8 g) of chilled meat filling to the dough and pinch up the sides to close. If you need a little extra dough, you can add more. Repeat until all dough is used up, making 12 to 14 balls.

In a small skillet, heat your fat of choice over medium heat until shimmering, 3 to 5 minutes.

Using a slotted spoon, carefully add 4 or 5 balls to the fat. Turn the balls once every 1 to 2 minutes to brown on all sides, cooking for a total of 6 to 9 minutes. Transfer to a paper towel–lined plate and allow to cool for 3 to 5 minutes before serving. Keep cooking in batches until all the balls are fried.

Serve immediately. Pairs well with Mojo de Ajo (page 153).

AIP COMPLIANT: Used boiled and mashed yuca instead of the potatoes (you can omit the tapioca starch, as it is not necessary when using yuca). Omit the black pepper and use the AIP-compliant version of Carne Molida (page 95) as the filling.

ARAÑITAS DE PLÁTANO
SHREDDED FRIED PLANTAIN "SPIDERS"

Pan-Latin

Arañitas means "little spiders." When you see all the spindly little "legs" that the plantain shreds form once you fry this dish, you will see why they were given such a name. Rather than adding seasoning to the fritters themselves, they are best dipped in your favorite flavorful sauce from the final chapter, "Los Esenciales."

MAKES 12 FRITTERS

2 green plantains, peeled and grated into large shreds

About ¼ cup (56 g) fat of choice for frying (lard or avocado oil recommended)

Fine Himalayan salt, to taste

Peel the plantains by slicing off both tips with a knife, then cut 1 or 2 slits in the skin down the length of the plantain. If the peel does not lift off easily, you can soak the plantains in a bowl covered with water and with about 1 teaspoon (6 g) of salt for 10 to 15 minutes to loosen the skin.

Use the large side of a box grater to shred the plantain. You can angle the plantain to create longer shreds, if desired. Do not use the fine grater or the texture will not be correct.

In a small or medium skillet, heat your fat of choice over medium heat for 3 to 5 minutes. The deeper the level of fat in your pan, the "fluffier" your *arañitas* will be. Using less fat results in flatter *arañitas*.

Divide the plantain shreds into 12 equal portions, shaping each portion into a ball between your hands and gently flattening before dropping them in the heated fat. Cook them for 3 to 4 minutes per side, or until golden and crispy. Work in batches as necessary. Transfer to a paper towel-lined plate.

Sprinkle with salt to taste and serve with your favorite dipping sauce, such as the Salsa Verde Mágica (page 165), Ajilimójili Sauce (page 151) or Guasacaca (page 166).

AIP COMPLIANT: No adjustments necessary!

RÁPIDO Y FÁCIL

QUICK AND EASY MEALS

Everyone loves to have a nice variety of delicious recipes tucked away in a back pocket that are both easy to make and fast to prepare. Although a lot of traditional Latin American fare can be quite labor-intensive and time-consuming, there are plenty of options that will allow you to get a meal on the table in 30 minutes or less without sacrificing flavor. These recipes are also quite versatile in terms of scalability. Many of these recipes, as written, are perfect for couples, but are scaled up easily to feed a crowd in a hurry or to save some in the freezer for batch cooking.

Picadillo, recipe on page 96.

PINCHOS DE POLLO
MARINATED GRILLED CHICKEN KEBABS

 Puerto Rico

Pinchos are traditional street food in Puerto Rico and can be made from pork or chicken that has been marinated in a tangy sauce and then grilled to perfection. You can serve these as an appetizer or a light meal. Leftovers are great to put on top of a salad, too!

SERVES 3 TO 4

1 tbsp (10 g) minced garlic

½ tsp fine Himalayan salt

½ tsp freshly ground black pepper

2 tsp (2 g) minced fresh oregano, or 1 tsp (2 g) dried

1 tbsp (15 ml) extra-virgin olive oil

1 tbsp (15 ml) freshly squeezed lime juice (from about ½ lime)

1½ lb (680 g) boneless, skinless chicken breast

Have ready 7 to 9 skewers. If using wooden or bamboo skewers, soak them in water for at least 30 minutes before grilling.

In a bowl, combine the garlic, salt, pepper, oregano, oil and lime juice and stir to form a paste.

Cut chicken breasts into 1-inch (2.5-cm) chunks and place in a glass container with a lid. Pour the marinade over the chicken and stir to combine. Cover the chicken and refrigerate for a minimum of 2 hours, up to overnight.

Prepare a grill for direct cooking over medium heat (325 to 375°F [170 to 190°C]). Depending on the type of grill this may take 15 to 20 minutes.

Remove the chicken from the refrigerator and thread it onto the skewers, spreading each piece as flat as possible and leaving a very small space between each piece.

Once the grill is hot, brush the cooking grates clean, if necessary (to prevent sticking). Grill the kebabs over direct medium heat, keeping the lid closed as much as possible, until the chicken is firm to the touch and no longer pink in the center, 8 to 10 minutes total, turning once or twice during cooking. Take care not overcook.

Remove from the grill and serve immediately. Pairs wonderfully with Tostones (page 115), and you can make mini sandwiches by placing one chunk of chicken between 2 *tostones*.

AIP COMPLIANT: Omit the black pepper.

REINA PEPIADA
CHICKEN AVOCADO SALAD

Venezuela

Reina pepiada is a dish that was meant to be fit for a queen—a beauty queen, that is. The 1955 winner of the Miss World Pageant was the first woman from Venezuela (or anywhere in South America, for that matter) to ever win the title, and a restaurant owner in Caracas created this dish to serve the winner. It is now arguably the most popular filling for arepas, for good reason!

SERVES 4

1 ripe Hass avocado, peeled and sliced

Juice of 1 lime

4 tbsp (4 g) chopped fresh cilantro

1 small yellow onion, minced

½ tsp fine Himalayan salt

Freshly ground black pepper, to taste

4 tbsp (56 g) Salsa de Ajo (page 157), or plain mayonnaise plus 1 clove garlic, minced

2 cups (280 g) Simple Shredded Chicken (page 167)

Place the avocado in a medium bowl and squeeze the lime juice on top. Use a fork or a potato masher to mash the avocado until creamy. Add all the remaining ingredients and mix well.

Cover and place in refrigerator for at least 1 hour before serving.

Stuff generously inside a fresh Venezuelan-style arepa (page 68) or on top of a Colombian-style arepa (page 67) or serve it on top of Tostones (page 115). It can also be served alone as a delicious and flavorful chicken salad.

AIP COMPLIANT: Omit the black pepper and use egg-free *Salsa de Ajo* (page 157), or omit if desired. Add 1 clove of garlic, minced. When I was AIP, I made this dish often without the mayonnaise. I also enjoyed adding something completely nontraditional yet delicious: 4 to 5 strips of crispy bacon, crumbled.

POLLO EN SOFRITO PARA EL AIP
CHICKEN IN SOFRITO FOR THE AIP

Puerto Rico

When I was living in Miami and strictly following the Paleo Autoimmune Protocol (AIP), I used to make this chicken all the time. While it is not technically a traditional Puerto Rican dish per se, it still tastes authentically Puerto Rican, thanks to the *sofrito*, and is a dish I'm sure you'll love to add to your rotation, too. You can also deviate a bit from tradition and bulk it up with additional AIP-compliant vegetables of choice, such as carrots or zucchini. Use this recipe instead of the Pollo Desmechado (page 98) for an AIP-compliant arepa topping.

SERVES 4 TO 6

3 tbsp (45 ml) extra-virgin olive oil

4 tbsp (55 g) AIP-compliant Sofrito (page 148)

1 medium onion, diced

2 cups (260 g) diced carrot, zucchini or other AIP-approved vegetable (optional)

4 to 6 cloves garlic, minced

1 tsp (6 g) fine Himalayan salt

1 tsp (2 g) dried oregano

Juice of 1 lime

2 tbsp (30 g) pure pumpkin puree, to thicken the sauce (optional)

2 cups (280 g) Simple Shredded Chicken (page 167), or 2 lb (905 g) boneless, skinless chicken breast, cut into 1" to 1½" (2.5 to 4 cm) pieces

Chopped fresh cilantro, for garnish

In a large skillet over medium heat, heat the olive oil. Add the *sofrito* and cook until the *sofrito* is fragrant, 2 to 4 minutes (longer if cooking with frozen *sofrito*). If using shredded chicken, first add the onion and cook for 3 to 4 minutes, stirring occasionally. If using additional veggies, add them with the onion. Add the garlic and cook for 2 minutes more. Add all the remaining ingredients, except the cilantro, and cook for an additional 10 minutes, or until the onion and additional veggies, if using, are tender and the chicken is warmed throughout.

If using raw chicken, add it to the pan with the *sofrito* and allow to cook, stirring occasionally, until all the chicken pieces are white on the outside, 5 to 7 minutes. Add all the remaining ingredients, including the veggies (if using) and cook for an additional 6 to 8 minutes, or until the chicken is cooked through and the vegetables are tender.

Garnish with chopped cilantro and serve as a main dish on its own or in a variety of other recipes: as a filling for Alcapurrias (page 60), on top of Arepas Colombianas (page 67), stuffed inside Carimañolas (page 71), as a filling for Pastelillos (page 55) or Empanadas al Horno (page 50) or stuffed inside Arepas Rellenas (page 68).

CANOAS DE PLÁTANOS MADUROS
MEAT-STUFFED RIPE PLANTAINS

 Puerto Rico

Canoas means "canoes" in Spanish, and as you will see, this is due to the look of the finished dish: The sweet plantains are turned into little canoes filled with delicious meat! This dish has such a fun presentation and can be made without a lot of fuss. It is one that my husband remembers fondly from his childhood and loves for me to make today.

SERVES 4 TO 6

6 ripe to very ripe plantains, peeled (yellow with some black)

About ¼ cup (56 g) fat for frying (lard, coconut oil or avocado oil), plus more for baking dish

½ batch Carne Molida (page 95)

"Queso" Blanco (page 170) or "Queso" Amarillo (page 169), to top (optional)

Chopped fresh cilantro, for garnish

Slice the tips off the plantains and cut a slit down the length of the peel and lift to remove.

In a medium skillet, heat your fat of choice over medium heat until shimmering, 3 to 5 minutes. Working in batches if necessary, carefully add the plantains to the heated fat (they should sizzle when dropped in), cooking on each side for 3 to 5 minutes, or until they have turned a nice golden brown and have partially caramelized. Be careful not to burn. Drain on a paper towel–lined plate.

Preheat the oven to 350°F (177°C).

Lightly grease the bottom of a 9 x 13-inch (23 x 33-cm) glass baking dish with coconut oil or lard. When the plantains have cooled enough to handle, place them so that the curved ends are pointing up and cut a slit down the length of each plantain along the center, being careful not to cut all the way through. Arrange them in the bottom of the dish and stuff generously with the meat filling. Bake for 15 to 20 minutes. If desired, top with pieces of the "Queso" Blanco for the last 5 to 7 minutes of baking or the "Queso" Amarillo for the last 1 to 2 minutes only. Sprinkle chopped cilantro on top and serve immediately.

AIP COMPLIANT: Use the AIP-compliant version of Carne Molida (page 95).

MOJO CHULETAS DE PUERCO
CITRUS MARINATED PORK CHOPS

 Cuba

Mojo Criollo (page 154) and pork are such a match made in heaven! Although this dish does require an overnight marinade, the actual hands-on time is minimal and this dish is quick to cook. Be sure to make these at your next cookout to wow your guests with the intense flavor!

SERVES 6

1 cup (235 ml) Mojo Criollo (page 154), divided

6 bone-in pork chops, ¾" to 1" [2 to 2.5 cm] thick (about 3 lb [1.4 kg])

1 medium onion, thinly sliced

1 tbsp (15 ml) extra-virgin olive oil

2 limes, cut into wedges

Reserve about ¼ cup (60 ml) of the *mojo criollo* in a covered container in the refrigerator.

Place the pork chops in a glass baking dish in a single layer and pour the remaining ¾ cup (175 ml) of marinade on top, covering both sides of each chop. Cover and refrigerate for a minimum of 2 hours or up to overnight for the most flavor.

Remove the pork chops from the refrigerator 30 minutes before grilling. Gently pat the pork chops dry and discard their marinade.

Prepare the grill for direct cooking over medium-high heat (375 to 400°F [190 to 200°C]), or heat a large grill pan over medium-high heat on the stovetop. Place the pork chops on the hot grill grates. Grill the pork chops 3 to 4 minutes per side, until browned and the center of the pork is no longer pink. The pork chops are done when the pork's internal temperature (using a meat thermometer) reaches 160°F (71°C).

While the pork is grilling, sauté the onion in the olive oil until it is translucent. Set aside.

Transfer the pork chops to a serving platter. Top with the sautéed onion and drizzle with the reserved *mojo criollo*. Serve with the lime wedges.

AIP COMPLIANT: Use the AIP-compliant version of Mojo Criollo (page 154).

"ARROZ" CON POLLO
CHICKEN WITH "RICE"

Puerto Rico

Arroz con pollo—chicken with rice—is true comfort food in many Latin American countries. On page 29 you will find a traditional home-style version from Milagros's family that includes white rice, but this version is a much quicker option, thanks to the shredded chicken, and adheres to strict Paleo by using cauliflower to replace the rice.

SERVES 4

1 head cauliflower

¼ cup (60 ml) extra-virgin olive oil

4 tbsp (55 g) Sofrito (page 148)

2 tsp (4 g) ground turmeric

1 tsp (6 g) fine Himalayan salt

1 red bell pepper, diced

1 small onion, diced

2 to 3 cups (280 to 420 g) Simple Shredded Chicken (page 167)

¼ cup (44 g) sliced green olives

Remove the stem and outer leaves from the cauliflower and cut it into several smaller chunks. In a food processor fitted with the blade attachment, pulse the cauliflower for about 10 seconds. Scrape down the sides and continue to pulse until all the cauliflower is riced, working in batches if necessary.

In a large skillet, heat the olive oil over medium heat. Add the *sofrito* and cook until it is fragrant, 2 to 4 minutes (longer if cooking with frozen *sofrito*).

Add the turmeric, salt, bell pepper, onion and shredded chicken and cook, stirring frequently, for about 3 minutes. Add the cauliflower and cook for 5 to 7 minutes more, until the cauliflower is cooked throughout and the pepper and onion are tender. Stir in the olives just before removing the pan from the heat.

NOTE: If you do not have a food processor, you can grate the cauliflower with a box grater instead. The pieces won't be as uniform, but it will still work!

AIP COMPLIANT: Use the AIP-compliant version of Sofrito (page 148) and omit the red bell pepper. Add 2 to 3 cloves of garlic, minced, after the *sofrito* is fragrant and cook for about 1 extra minute.

"VACA" FRITA DE POLLO
GARLIC-LIME FRIED SHREDDED CHICKEN

Cuba

Translating the name of this dish is a bit nonsensical since it would be "fried cow of chicken," but it is simply a version of the classic Vaca Frita (page 19)—"fried cow"—made with chicken instead of beef. I like to keep plain shredded cooked chicken on hand in my freezer so I can use it to quickly make meals like this or Reina Pepiada (page 84). See Simple Shredded Chicken (page 167) for how to cook the chicken in bulk on the stovetop, in a slow cooker or in a pressure cooker.

SERVES 4

2 cups (280 g) Simple Shredded Chicken (page 167)

¼ cup (60 ml) freshly squeezed lime juice

1 tbsp (10 g) minced garlic

1 tsp (6 g) fine Himalayan salt

4 to 6 tbsp (56 to 84 g) fat of choice for frying (lard, avocado oil or extra-virgin olive oil)

1 white onion, cut into thin rings

Lime wedges, for garnish

In a mixing bowl, combine the shredded chicken, lime juice, garlic and salt and stir well. You can let it marinate for 30 to 60 minutes in the refrigerator or cook it right away if you're in a hurry.

In a large skillet, heat your fat of choice over medium heat until shimmering, 3 to 5 minutes. Add the chicken and spread into a thin even layer in the pan. Let it fry undisturbed for 10 to 15 minutes, or until it is browned and crispy on the bottom. This may seem like a long time, but it is correct.

Add additional cooking fat as needed. Stir the chicken and let it fry undisturbed for another 5 minutes. Add the onion rings and stir to mix in with the chicken, frying for an additional 5 to 10 minutes while stirring occasionally. The end result should be crispy and browned and the onion softened but not mushy. Garnish with lime wedges and serve.

AIP COMPLIANT: No changes necessary!

CARNE MOLIDA
GROUND BEEF HASH

Puerto Rico

Carne molida translates as "ground meat," but don't let the simple name fool you into thinking it is a boring dish! It is easy to throw together on a busy weeknight and is full of flavor, thanks to the *sofrito* cooking base. This is how Milagros learned to make this dish in Puerto Rico. You can serve this as a quick main protein or use it as a filling for Canoas de Plátanos Maduros (page 87), Alcapurrias (page 60) or Pastelillos (page 55). This dish also freezes well if you make a double batch.

SERVES 6 TO 8

2 tbsp (30 ml) extra-virgin olive oil

4 tbsp (55 g) Sofrito (page 148)

2 large cloves garlic, minced

½ tsp fine Himalayan salt

½ tsp freshly ground black pepper

1 small onion, diced

2 lb (905 g) ground beef

2 tbsp (32 g) tomato paste

1 medium yellow potato, cut into ½" (1.3-cm) dice

½ cup (65 g) diced carrot

12 to 15 green Manzanilla olives, sliced

In a large sauté pan with a lid, heat the olive oil over medium heat for 1 to 2 minutes. Add the *sofrito*, garlic, salt and pepper and cook, stirring, 2 to 4 minutes, until sizzling and fragrant (longer if using frozen *sofrito*).

Add all the remaining ingredients, except the olives. Cook for about 10 minutes, until the meat is browned, stirring occasionally to break up the meat.

Lower the heat to low or medium-low to bring the mixture to a simmer, cover and cook for 20 to 30 minutes more, until the potatoes and carrot are tender when pierced with a fork.

AIP COMPLIANT: Use the AIP-compliant version of Sofrito (page 148), omit the black pepper and substitute diced green plantain, taro, yuca, malanga or *ñame* for the potatoes.

PICADILLO

SWEET AND SAVORY GROUND BEEF

 Cuba

Picadillo has such an interesting contrast of flavors and is well spiced without being hot. You don't often think to pair raisins or "sweet" spices like allspice with ground beef, but it works incredibly well in this dish to balance the umami from the tomatoes, olives and capers. Use *picadillo* as a quick and easy main dish or as a filling for Mini Papas Rellenas (page 76).

SERVES 4 TO 6

2 tbsp (30 ml) extra-virgin olive oil

1 cup (150 g) diced red bell pepper

1 cup (160 g) diced onion

2 tbsp (20 g) minced garlic (about 1 whole head)

2 lb (905 g) ground beef

1½ tsp (4 g) ground cumin

1½ tsp (3 g) dried oregano

1 tsp (2 g) ground allspice

1½ tsp (9 g) fine Himalayan salt

3 tbsp (48 g) tomato paste

2 tbsp (17 g) drained capers

⅓ cup (33 g) sliced green Manzanilla olives

⅓ cup (50 g) raisins

¼ cup (4 g) chopped fresh cilantro or flat-leaf parsley

In a large sauté pan with a lid, heat the olive oil over medium heat for 1 to 2 minutes. Add the bell pepper and onion and cook until the onion is translucent, 4 to 5 minutes. Add the garlic and cook for about 2 minutes more. Add the ground beef and cook until browned, about 15 minutes, stirring occasionally and breaking up all the chunks.

Next, add all the remaining ingredients, except the cilantro, and stir well to combine. Lower the heat, cover and cook for about 15 more minutes, or until the sauce has thickened.

Turn off the heat and stir in the cilantro. Serve with your favorite side dishes.

See image on page 80.

AIP COMPLIANT: This dish is difficult to make AIP compliant while retaining authentic flavor. You can make it nightshade-free by omitting the bell pepper and replacing the tomato paste with canned pumpkin puree. Replace the allspice with ½ teaspoon of cinnamon, ½ teaspoon of ground cloves and ¼ teaspoon of mace. Use this as a reintroduction recipe for cumin, as there is no AIP replacement.

BISTEC DE PALOMILLA
THIN-CUT STEAK AND ONIONS

 Cuba

Palomilla steaks are very common in Cuban restaurants. They are cut ultrathin from sirloin steaks or top round, marinated and then cooked ultrafast. The key is to have the meat no more than ¼-inch (6-mm) thick so that you can cook them in under 5 minutes flat over high heat. If you live near a Cuban butcher, they will likely sell these sliced steaks, but ask them if they will slice your prefered cut for you. Otherwise, cut them at home yourself (see note).

SERVES 4

4 large cloves garlic, minced

Juice of 2 limes

½ tsp fine Himalayan salt

4 sirloin or top round steaks, cut to ¼" (6 mm) thick and weighing about 8 oz (225 g) each

2 tbsp (30 ml) avocado oil (do not substitute another oil)

1 onion, thinly sliced

¼ cup (15 g) chopped fresh parsley, for garnish

In a small bowl, combine the garlic, lime juice and salt. Place the steaks in a single layer in a glass dish with a lid and cover with the lime marinade. Cover the dish and refrigerate for 15 to 60 minutes. Do not marinate for longer than 1 hour. Due to the thinness of the steak, a longer marinade can tenderize the meat too much and result in an unpleasant texture. While your steak is marinating, prepare your side dishes of choice.

In a large skillet, heat the avocado oil over high heat for 2 to 3 minutes. You want the pan to be very hot and to hear those steaks sizzle loudly as soon as they hit the pan. Cook the steaks in 2 batches if necessary; do not overcrowd the pan. Rapidly cook the meat for 1 to 2 minutes per side, until both sides are seared. Remove with a slotted spoon and set aside.

Lower the heat to medium and add the onion, cooking until it is softened but still crunchy, 3 to 5 minutes. Turn off the heat and stir in the parsley. Serve the steaks immediately with a generous portion of the onion mixture.

NOTE: Cut the steaks into thin slices if you were not able to buy them already sliced. One trick to make cutting meat easier is to partially freeze it for 30 to 60 minutes before cutting. It does take some skill, a steady hand and a good knife to cut the steak to only ¼ inch (6 mm) thick. Work carefully and if your steaks slices turn out thicker, simply place between 2 pieces of plastic wrap and pound with the flat side of a meat mallet until they are ¼-inch (6-mm) thick.

AIP COMPLIANT: No changes necessary!

POLLO DESMECHADO
SEASONED SHREDDED CHICKEN

Colombia

This shredded chicken tastes just like the chicken at my favorite Colombian restaurant here in Memphis. I love how incredibly fast and easy it is to throw this dish together on a busy day and it is amazing just how versatile it is—check out the list of recipes you can use it in!

SERVES 4 TO 6

3 tbsp (45 ml) extra-virgin olive oil

2 large yellow or orange bell peppers, diced

1 small onion, diced

4 to 6 cloves garlic, minced

2 tbsp (32 g) tomato paste

2 plum tomatoes, diced

1 tsp (6 g) fine Himalayan salt

½ tsp freshly ground black pepper

½ tsp ground cumin

½ tsp paprika

2 cups (280 g) Simple Shredded Chicken (page 167)

Chopped fresh cilantro, for garnish

In a large skillet, heat the olive oil over medium heat for 2 to 3 minutes. Add the bell peppers and onion and cook for 3 to 4 minutes, stirring occasionally. Add the garlic and cook for 2 minutes more. Add all the remaining ingredients, except the cilantro, stir to combine and cook for an additional 10 minutes, or until the vegetables are tender and the chicken is warmed throughout.

Garnish with the cilantro and serve as a main dish on its own, on top of Arepas Colombianas (page 67) or stuffed inside Carimañolas (page 71). You can also mix cuisines and use it as a filling for Pastelillos (page 55) or Empanadas al Horno (page 50) or stuffed inside Arepas Rellenas (page 68).

AIP COMPLIANT: See the Pollo en Sofrito para el AIP (page 85).

POLLO A LA PLANCHA
MARINATED GRILLED CHICKEN BREAST

Pan-Latin

"Chicken on the grill" may sound plain, but this dish is so perfectly seasoned you'll never think grilled chicken is boring again. The color of the cooked chicken is also exquisite and makes for a beautiful, delicious meal you can cook on any busy weeknight. Make a double batch to have leftovers for salads!

SERVES 2

2 boneless, skinless chicken breasts

½ tsp ground paprika

¼ tsp granulated garlic

¼ tsp granulated onion

¼ to ½ tsp ground cumin

¼ tsp fine Himalayan salt

Zest and juice of 1 lime

1½ tsp (8 ml) extra-virgin olive oil

Prepare a grill for direct cooking over medium heat (325 to 375°F [170 to 190°C]). Depending on type of grill, this may take 15 to 20 minutes.

While the grill is heating, wrap the breasts in a layer of plastic wrap and use a flat meat mallet or the bottom of a sturdy glass or jar to pound the breasts to a uniform thickness of about ½ inch (1.3 cm).

Combine the remaining ingredients in a bowl and stir to form a paste. Coat the pounded breasts with the mixture.

Once the grill is hot, brush the cooking grates clean, if necessary (to prevent sticking). Grill the chicken breasts over direct medium heat, with the lid closed as much as possible, until the meat is firm to the touch and no longer pink in the center, 8 to 12 minutes total, turning once or twice.

Remove from the grill and let rest for 3 to 5 minutes before serving.

> **AIP COMPLIANT:** Omit the paprika and cumin, add ¼ teaspoon of ground turmeric and double the amount of granulated garlic and onion.

ANTICUCHOS DE CORAZÓN

MARINATED BEEF HEART KEBABS

Peru

Beef heart is an excellent choice if you are new to eating offal, because it tastes like a fine steak. If you are lucky, your butcher will be able to sell you cleaned and cut heart rather than an entire heart. This traditional Peruvian dish marinates the heart in a delicious sauce that you can actually use to marinate any cut of meat. If you are too squeamish to cook heart, you can use any steak or even cubed chicken breast instead. But I highly recommend that you give beef heart a chance!

SERVES 2 TO 4

½ cup (120 ml) freshly squeezed lime juice

3 to 4 tbsp (48 to 64 g) *ají panca* paste (see note for substitutes)

6 cloves garlic, peeled and minced

1½ tsp (9 g) fine Himalayan salt

1 tsp (2 g) freshly ground black pepper

1 tsp (3 g) ground cumin powder

4 tbsp (60 ml) extra-virgin olive oil, divided

1 lb (455 g) beef heart, trimmed

Combine the lime juice, *ají panca* paste, garlic, salt, black pepper, cumin and 2 tablespoons (30 ml) of the olive oil in a glass container with a lid.

If not already cleaned, trim the heart of fat, connective tissue and blood vessels. Cut the meat into equal-size chunks, 1 to 2 inches (2.5 to 5 cm) across and ½ inch (1.3 cm) thick.

Place the heart chunks in the marinade and toss to combine. Cover and refrigerate for a minimum of 1 hour, up to overnight.

Before grilling, have ready 6 to 8 skewers. If using wooden or bamboo skewers, soak them in water for at least 30 minutes.

Meanwhile, prepare the grill for direct cooking over medium heat (325 to 375°F [170 to 190°C]). Depending on type of grill, this may take 15 to 20 minutes.

Thread the heart pieces onto the skewers. Make sure each piece is spread as flat as possible and leave a very small space between each piece.

Once the grill is hot, brush the cooking grates clean, if necessary (to prevent sticking). Grill the skewers over direct medium heat for 2 to 3 minutes per side for medium rare or 4 to 5 minutes for medium well done. Brush the kebabs with the remaining olive oil at least once during cooking. Do not overcook or else the beef heart will become tough and rubbery.

Serve immediately as an appetizer or with your favorite sides for a meal. This pairs very well with Tostones (page 115).

AIP COMPLIANT: Omit the *ají panca* paste, black pepper and the cumin. You can replace them with 2 tablespoons (30 g) of the AIP-compliant version of Sofrito (page 148) if you like, but the kebabs taste great without it, too.

NOTE: *Ají panca* paste can be ordered online if you can't find it locally, or you can substitute 1 to 2 tablespoons (7.5 to 15 g) of *pasilla* or ancho chile powder. Taste the marinade before adding the meat and adjust to your preferred level of spiciness.

CHURRASCO
GRILLED SKIRT STEAK

Argentina

When I lived in Miami Beach, my neighborhood was called "Little Argentina." I had the privilege of living down the street from an incredible Argentinean steakhouse where I was first introduced to *churrasco* steak, which refers to grilled skirt steak. I also befriended several neighbors in my condo building who hailed from Argentina and enjoyed many *churrasco* grilling sessions with them on our back patio. *Churrasco* is extremely simple—all you need is skirt steak and salt. Pair it with *chimichurri* sauce for an incredible meal perfect to share with friends.

SERVES 4

2 lb (905 g) skirt steak (each steak is usually 1 lb [455 g])

1 tsp (6 g) fine Himalayan salt

Chimichurri (page 158) to serve

Prepare a grill for direct cooking over medium heat (325 to 375°F [170 to 190°C]). Depending on type of grill, this may take 15 to 20 minutes.

Immediately before grilling, rub both sides of the steak with salt. Cook the steak for 3 to 5 minutes per side for medium rare.

Transfer to a plate and let stand for 5 minutes. Slice into 1- to 2-inch (2.5- to 5-cm) strips across the grain at an angle and serve generously topped with *chimichurri*.

AIP COMPLIANT: Use the AIP-compliant version of Chimichurri (page 158).

ACOMPAÑANTES

SIDES

Throughout Latin America the typical accompaniments to meals are a delightful array of tropical starchy fruits, roots and tubers cooked with flavorful sauces. If you are not already familiar with plantains, yuca, green bananas and boniato, you will soon fall in love with these ingredients to broaden the variety in your diet.

And of course, since rice and beans are such staple side dishes, I have included both a starchy and a non-starchy replacement option for each of these so that you have Paleo-friendly options to round out your meals.

Guineitos en Escabeche, recipe on page 121.

PAPAS A LA HUANCAÍNA
POTATOES IN "CHEESE" SAUCE

 Peru

Adapting this traditional Peruvian dish to be both grain-free and dairy-free was a feat, since the sauce is normally made with both cheese and cream and thickened with cracker crumbs. My husband told me that my "cheese" sauce is frighteningly authentic, and I think you'll agree. Some like to really turn up the heat in this dish, but it's up to you how hot to make the sauce.

SERVES 4 TO 6

2 to 2½ lb (905 g to 1.1 kg) Yukon gold potatoes, peeled

FOR THE "CHEESE" SAUCE

1 cup (235 ml) Chicken Broth (page 168)

4 tbsp (28 g) unflavored gelatin

1 cup (235 ml) canned full-fat coconut milk

2 tbsp (30 ml) extra-virgin olive oil

¼ cup (32 g) nutritional yeast

1½ tsp (7 ml) red palm oil, for color

½ tsp ground turmeric

1 tsp (6 g) fine Himalayan salt

½ to 3 tbsp (5 to 27 g) minced *ají amarillo* or another chile pepper (see note)

1 tsp (2 g) granulated onion

1 tsp (3 g) granulated garlic

2 tbsp (30 ml) apple cider vinegar

2 tbsp (16 g) tapioca starch dissolved in 2 tbsp (30 ml) water

FOR SERVING

2 to 3 large hard boiled eggs, peeled and sliced

4 to 6 leaves romaine lettuce

¼ cup (25 g) sliced black olives (Peruvian *botija* olives are ideal)

Sprig of curly-leaf parsley, for garnish

Begin by cooking the potatoes. Place the peeled potatoes in a 4-quart (3.8-L) or larger pot and cover with water. Bring to a boil over high heat, then lower the heat to a gentle boil and cover, cooking until the potatoes are tender, 25 to 30 minutes.

Meanwhile, prepare the "cheese" sauce. Pour the chicken broth into a medium pot. Slowly sprinkle the gelatin, about 1½ teaspoons (3.5 g) at a time, on top of the broth to "bloom" it. Do this slowly so that clumps do not form. Once all of the gelatin has been added, heat the pot over medium heat until the gelatin has dissolved.

Whisk in all the remaining sauce ingredients and cook for about 5 minutes. Remember to make a slurry by combining the tapioca starch with the water before adding it to the pot, otherwise it won't dissolve evenly.

Reduce the heat to low and cover, to keep it warm until the dish is ready to serve.

Meanwhile, prepare the serving ingredients. Hard-boil the eggs by placing them in a pot with a lid and covering with at least 1 inch (2.5 cm) of water. Heat, uncovered, over high heat until the water reaches a rolling boil, then cover with the lid and turn off the heat, but leave on the burner. Let sit for 10 to 12 minutes, then drain and run the eggs under cool water.

Drain the potatoes and place in a bowl or on a plate. Carefully, without burning your fingers, slice the potatoes crosswise into 3 or 4 slices each.

To assemble the dish, arrange the lettuce leaves on your serving dish. Layer the potato slices evenly on top of the leaves. Pour the warm cheese sauce on top. Garnish with sliced hard-boiled eggs, olives and a sprig of parsley. Serve immediately.

AIP COMPLIANT: Substitute boiled and drained yuca (see Yuca con Mojo [page 123] for directions) for the potatoes and simply omit the chile pepper from the cheese sauce as well as the eggs from the final dish.

PLÁTANOS MADUROS
FRIED RIPE PLANTAINS

Pan-Latin

Maduros are made from very ripe plantains that are a blend of yellow and black (not yet mostly black) and are a staple side dish throughout Latin America. They are one of my favorite starchy sides to go with just about anything. I love the way the natural sugars caramelize during cooking to provide a lovely sweet contrast to any savory main dish.

SERVES 2 TO 3

2 ripe or very ripe plantains (yellow and black; should give when pressed but not be mushy)

2 to 4 tbsp (28 to 56 g) fat of choice (coconut oil recommended, but lard, ghee and avocado oil also work)

Coarse sea salt, for garnish

To peel ripe plantains, first slice off both tips with a knife, then cut a slit in the skin down the length of the plantain. Lift off the peel with your fingers.

You can cut the plantains one of two ways: into disks about ¾-inch (2-cm) thick or on the bias (diagonally) into oblong strips about ½-inch (1.3-cm) thick. The latter option results in a more visually interesting dish and is likely how you have been served *maduros* at a restaurant.

In a large skillet, heat your fat of choice over medium heat until shimmering, 3 to 5 minutes. Carefully add the slices to the heated fat (they should sizzle when dropped in), cooking on each side for 3 to 5 minutes, or until they have turned a nice golden brown and have partially caramelized. Be careful not to burn.

Serve immediately with any main dish.

AIP COMPLIANT: No adjustments necessary!

MANGÚ CON CEBOLLA
MASHED GREEN PLANTAINS WITH ONIONS

 Dominican Republic

Mangú is a ubiquitous side dish in the Dominican Republic and you will often find it served with eggs and salami for breakfast. However, it pairs well with just about any main dish in this cookbook. The "pickled" onion topping provides a wonderful contrast of flavor for this hearty, sticks-to-your-ribs side dish. You can even use the onions to garnish steak or pork chops, too!

SERVES 4 TO 6

FOR THE *MANGÚ*

4 green plantains, peeled and cut

1 tsp (6 g) plus 1 pinch of fine Himalayan salt, divided

¼ cup (60 ml) extra-virgin olive oil, butter (if tolerated), lard or ghee

½ cup (120 ml) cold water

FOR THE *CEBOLLA*

2 tbsp (30 ml) extra-virgin olive oil

1 large red onion, cut into thin slices

1 tsp (6 g) fine Himalayan salt

2 tbsp (30 ml) distilled white vinegar or coconut vinegar

Prepare the *mangú*. To peel green plantains, first slice off both tips with a knife, then cut 1 or 2 slits in the skin down the length of the plantain. If the peel does not lift off easily you can loosen it by soaking the plantains in a bowl of water with about 1 tablespoon (6 g) of salt for 10 to 15 minutes.

Cut the peeled plantains in half through the center and then cut each piece in half lengthwise. Place in a pot and cover with 1 inch (2.5 cm) of water plus the pinch of salt and heat over high heat until boiling. Boil for 20 to 25 minutes, or until the plantains are fork-tender.

Meanwhile, prepare the *cebolla*. In a large skillet, heat the olive oil over medium heat. Add the sliced onion and salt and sauté until the onion is tender, about 5 minutes. Reduce the heat to low and stir in the vinegar. Keep warm over low heat until ready to serve with the *mangú*.

Once the plantains are tender, drain them and place in a large mixing bowl. Add your fat of choice and 1 teaspoon (6 g) of salt. Use a potato masher or a sturdy fork to mash the plantains. After the fat has combined with the plantains, add the cold water and continue to mash for another minute or two, until it forms a nice creamy consistency. Using cold water supposedly improves the texture of the mashed plantains and helps them stay soft when reheating leftovers. If necessary, you can add extra water ¼ cup (60 ml) at a time, until the texture is very smooth.

Serve the *mangú* with a generous portion of *cebolla* on top.

Store leftovers in the fridge in an airtight container. You can reheat leftovers in a covered dish in the oven.

AIP COMPLIANT: No adjustments necessary!

TOSTONES/PATACONES
TWICE-FRIED GREEN PLANTAINS

Pan-Latin

Green plantains that are fried, smashed and fried again are called *tostones* in some parts of Latin America and *patacones* in others. To make preparing these crispy bits of starchy deliciousness much easier, I recommend spending a few dollars on what is called a *tostone* press, which you can order online or pick up at your local Latin American grocery store. You can also use a sturdy glass or jar or even a flat meat mallet, too. *Tostones* can go well with just about any main dish or can be eaten as an appetizer or snack—think of them as hearty chips.

SERVES 2 TO 3

2 green plantains

4 to 6 tbsp (56 to 84 g) fat of choice (coconut oil, lard or avocado oil)

Coarse sea salt

1 to 2 tbsp (1 to 2 g) chopped fresh cilantro, for garnish

Mojo de Ajo (page 153) or Ajilimójili (page 151), for dipping

Slice the tips off the plantains with a knife, then cut 1 or 2 slits in the skin down the length of the plantain. If the peel does not lift off easily you can loosen it by soaking the plantains in a bowl of water with about 1 tablespoon (6 g) of salt for 10 to 15 minutes.

Slice the peeled plantain crosswise into disks ¾ to 1 inch (2 to 2.5 cm) wide.

In a large skillet, heat your fat of choice over medium heat until shimmering, 3 to 5 minutes. Carefully add the disks to the heated fat, cooking on each side for 2 to 4 minutes, or until they have turned a darker, more golden color. Do not allow to brown.

Remove the disks from the oil and flatten, using a *tostone* press (recommended) or a sturdy glass/jar or flat meat mallet. If using a *tostone* press, place the disk in the recessed circle and then clamp down the lid on top.

Return the flattened plantain disks to the hot oil and fry for an additional 2 to 3 minutes on each side, or until crispy and browned. You will likely need to work in batches to fry the flattened disks.

Add extra cooking fat as needed, because these will absorb quite a bit of fat as they cook.

Top with a sprinkling of coarse sea salt and a garnish of cilantro and serve immediately; *tostones* do not reheat well. Serve with Mojo de Ajo (page 153) or Ajilimójili Sauce (page 151) or with your favorite main dish.

AIP COMPLIANT: No adjustments necessary!

"ARROZ" AMARILLO DE COLIFLOR
YELLOW CAULIFLOWER "RICE"

 Puerto Rico

This is a grain-free, low-carb option for Puerto Rican style yellow "rice" that has all the flavor of the original dish but without the grains. It is extremely easy to prepare with the help of a good food processor and can be a really tasty way to pack more vegetables into your diet.

SERVES 6

1 head cauliflower

¼ cup (60 ml) extra-virgin olive oil

2 tbsp (30 g) Sofrito (page 148)

1½ tsp (3 g) ground turmeric

1 tsp (6 g) fine Himalayan salt

½ red bell pepper, diced (optional)

¼ cup (25 g) sliced green olives (optional)

Remove the stem and outer leaves from the cauliflower and cut it into several smaller chunks. In a food processor, using the blade attachment, pulse the cauliflower for about 10 seconds. Scrape down the sides and continue to pulse until all the cauliflower is riced, working in batches if necessary.

Heat the olive oil in a large (12-inch [30.5-cm]) skillet over medium heat. Add the *sofrito* and cook until it is fragrant, 2 to 4 minutes (longer if cooking with frozen *sofrito*).

Add the turmeric, salt and cauliflower and cook, stirring frequently, for about 3 minutes. Add the bell pepper and olives, if using, and cook for about 5 minutes more, until the cauliflower is cooked throughout and the bell pepper is tender.

NOTE: You can also grate the cauliflower with a box grater to "rice" it. The pieces won't be as uniform as they would be in a food processor, but it will still work!

AIP COMPLIANT: Do not include the red bell pepper and use the AIP-compliant version of Sofrito (page 148).

ARROZ AMARILLO
YELLOW RICE

Puerto Rico

This is a traditional dish with a nontraditional ingredient: turmeric. It is very common throughout Latin America to use annatto seeds to dye lard or olive oil to give classic dishes a distinctive yellow-orange color. It is purely for visual presentation and does not affect the flavor. Milagros prefers to use a little ground turmeric instead, since it offers major health benefits and is anti-inflammatory. The color turns out a bit more bright yellow, but it still feels festive! Again, as with the Home-Style Arroz con Pollo (page 29), I am including this version using white rice, but I've got two grain-free options for you that are both delicious: one low-carb (page 116) and one starchy (page 118).

SERVES 6 TO 8

2 tbsp (30 ml) extra-virgin olive oil

1 tbsp (15 g) Sofrito (page 148)

½ tsp fine Himalayan salt

½ tsp freshly ground black pepper

1 tsp (2 g) ground turmeric

1 cup (195 g) long-grain white rice, rinsed under running water until the water runs clear

2 cups (475 ml) Chicken Broth (page 168) or filtered water

In a Dutch oven or heavy-bottomed pot, heat the olive oil over medium heat for 1 to 2 minutes. Add the *sofrito*, salt, pepper and turmeric and cook, stirring, for 2 to 4 minutes (longer if cooking with frozen *sofrito*), until sizzling and fragrant.

Add the rice and broth, increase the heat to high to bring to a boil, then reduce the heat to low and cover. Cook for 10 to 12 minutes, or until no broth remains.

NOTE: White rice is not AIP compliant; however, it is a commonly tolerated reintroduction. Use the AIP-compliant version of Sofrito (page 148) to keep it nightshade-free.

"ARROZ" BLANCO O AMARILLO DE MALANGA

WHITE OR YELLOW MALANGA "RICE"

Pan-Latin

Cauliflower rice isn't everyone's cup of tea, and sometimes you really want (and need) something starchy to pair with your meals, so I developed this, which I dub the best Paleo rice replacement ever. It is made from the malanga root and is just as easy to make as cauli-rice and helps soak up the juices on your plate. You can serve this rice replacement without the seasoning if you want a plain white "rice" option with your meal and with dishes traditionally served with white rice, such as Lomo Saltado (page 20) and Pabellón Criollo (page 47).

SERVES 4

FOR PLAIN WHITE "RICE"
2 malanga roots or 1 small taro root (about 1 to 1½ lbs [450 to 680 g])

FOR PUERTO RICAN YELLOW "RICE"
2 tbsp (30 ml) olive oil
1 tbsp (15 g) Sofrito (page 148)
½ tsp fine Himalayan salt
1 tsp (2 g) ground turmeric
½ tsp freshly ground black pepper

AIP COMPLIANT: No adjustments needed for the white "rice"; use the AIP-compliant version of Sofrito (page 148) and omit the black pepper in the yellow "rice."

To prepare plain white "rice," peel the malanga roots and cut each into 4 or 5 large chunks.

Place a few chunks in a food processor and pulse for 8 to 10 seconds. Scrape down the sides with a spatula and remove any large pieces that did not begin to rice. Pulse for 8 to 10 more seconds, then empty the processor. Add any large chunks that were removed and repeat the process until the entire root is ground up. Be careful not to overprocess, otherwise it will turn the "rice" into more of a doughlike consistency.

Place a vegetable steamer basket in a pot with a lid and pour about 1 inch (2.5 cm) of water in the bottom of the pot. Heat it over high heat.

Place the riced malanga in the steamer basket, spreading it evenly over as much of the surface as you can. If it is a small basket, you may need to work in batches (you don't want the malanga layered too thick or the inside won't cook).

When the water boils, cover the pot with the lid and lower the heat to a low boil. Steam the malanga rice for about 10 minutes. About halfway through, carefully stir the malanga rice around to help with even cooking.

Carefully remove from the steamer basket and fluff the cooked malanga rice with 2 forks.

To make Puerto Rican–style yellow rice, while the malanga is steaming, heat the olive oil in a large skillet over medium heat for 1 to 2 minutes. Add the *sofrito*, salt, turmeric and black pepper and stir for 2 to 4 minutes (longer if cooking with frozen *sofrito*), until sizzling and fragrant. Add the cooked malanga rice to the pan and quickly stir to combine and coat it, letting the flavors combine for 30 to 60 seconds. Remove from the pan immediately and serve.

DULCE O SALADO PURÉ DE BONIATO
SWEET OR SAVORY MASHED BONIATO

 *Cuba & Puerto Rico*

This sweet root vegetable is a type of sweet potato commonly used in Latin America and goes by different names in different countries; when buying it in the United States, you will most often see it labeled as "boniato." It has a unique sweet flavor and a starchier, drier consistency than the yellow sweet potatoes we typically eat in the United States. It is quite versatile and can be made into a sweet or savory side dish, depending on your mood.

SERVES 4 TO 6

2 lb (905 g) boniato (also called *batata*)

FOR A SWEET MASH

1 (13.5-oz [399-ml]) can full-fat coconut milk

1 tsp (2 g) ground cinnamon

1 tsp (2 g) aniseeds

1 to 2 tbsp (15 to 30 g) sweetener (coconut sugar or honey work well) (optional)

FOR A SAVORY MASH

2 tbsp (30 ml) extra-virgin olive oil

1 small onion, diced

4 cloves garlic, minced

Juice of 2 limes

1 cup (235 ml) Chicken Broth (page 168)

1 tsp (2 g) dried oregano

1 tsp (6 g) fine Himalayan salt

Peel the boniato roots and cut into cubes about 2 inches (5 cm) across. Place in a pot and cover with water by 1 inch (2.5 cm). Bring to a boil over high heat, then lower the heat to a simmer and cover. Cook until the chunks are fork-tender, about 20 minutes.

Drain the cooked boniato to a large bowl. Since boniato can be fibrous inside, I recommend using an immersion blender or a food processor to make a smooth purée for the sweet version. You can also simply use a potato masher or even a sturdy fork for a chunkier consistency, if you prefer—this works well for the savory version.

For a sweet mash, combine the coconut milk with the cooked boniato and mash, then combine with the remaining sweet ingredients and mix well. Serve immediately.

For a savory mash, while the boniato is boiling, heat the olive oil in a pan over medium heat for 1 to 2 minutes, then add the onion and cook until translucent, 8 to 10 minutes. Add the garlic and continue to cook for an additional 1 to 2 minutes, until the garlic is fragrant. Turn off the heat and add the lime juice to the pan, stirring to scrape up any browned bits from the pan, mash the drained boniato with the chicken broth, then add the onion mixture and sprinkle the oregano and salt on top. Stir to combine well and serve immediately.

> **AIP COMPLIANT:** In the sweet mash, omit the aniseeds and optionally replace with ½ teaspoon of ground mace. The savory mash needs no adjustments.

GUINEITOS EN ESCABECHE
GREEN BANANAS IN OIL AND VINEGAR

 Puerto Rico

I never knew how versatile green bananas, called *guineitos*, could be before learning to cook Puerto Rican food. It turns out that you can make an incredible tamale-like dough from them (see Pasteles, page 33) and they also make a unique and delicious side dish. *Escabeche* refers to an ancient oil and vinegar method of preservation, but in the modern kitchen it serves as a flavorful marinade for the bananas.

SERVES 4 TO 6

5 to 6 green bananas

½ medium white onion, cut into rings

¼ cup (60 ml) coconut vinegar or distilled white vinegar

½ cup (120 ml) extra-virgin olive oil

½ tsp fine Himalayan salt

3 *ajíes dulces* or 1 small red bell pepper, diced

3 large cloves garlic, minced

6 whole black peppercorns

2 bay leaves

12 to 15 green Manzanilla olives (optional)

Cut the tips off the green bananas and cut 2 to 3 slits down the length of each peel. Place the bananas in a large pot and cover with water. Bring to a boil and cook for 15 to 20 minutes over medium-low heat, until the peels are easily removed and the bananas are tender. Take care not to overcook or the bananas will fall apart. Note that the cooking water may turn black, but this is normal.

In a bowl, cover the onion ring slices with the vinegar and set aside.

While the bananas are cooking, combine the oil, salt, *ajíes dulces*, garlic, peppercorns and bay leaves in a saucepan and cook over medium-low heat for about 20 minutes, to infuse the flavors into the oil. Do not allow the oil to get too hot. Just before draining the bananas, add the onion and vinegar (and olives, if using), increasing the heat to medium and cook for about 5 minutes, to lightly soften the onion.

Drain the bananas and allow to cool enough to handle. Remove the peel and slice into 1-inch (2.5-cm) disks. You may plunge them in an ice bath to quickly cool them, if desired.

Place the sliced bananas in a glass dish with a lid and pour the marinade on top. Cover and refrigerate several hours or overnight to allow the bananas to soak up the flavor. Serve chilled.

See image on page 106.

AIP COMPLIANT: Omit the peppers and peppercorns from the sauce and instead use 2 to 3 tablespoons (30 to 45 g) of the AIP-compliant version of Sofrito (page 148).

YUCA CON MOJO
BOILED YUCA WITH TANGY GARLIC SAUCE

Cuba

Yuca has a mild yet distinctive flavor that begs to be paired with a flavorful sauce. This humble root really comes alive when you let it simmer with tangy, garlicky *mojo criollo* sauce. You will find this dish on the menu at most Cuban restaurants and it will surely become a new family favorite.

SERVES 4

1½ to 2 lb (680 to 905 g) yuca (frozen works well)

Juice of 1 lime

½ tsp fine Himalayan salt

¾ cup (175 ml) Mojo Criollo (page 154)

1 small white or yellow onion, sliced into rings

If using fresh yuca, peel the root with a knife or sharp vegetable peeler, ensuring you remove all traces of the pink/purple layer just beneath the skin. Cut off both tips and cut the root crosswise into lengths of about 3 inches (7.5 cm). Inspect the flesh to ensure it is pure white with no soft spots, discolorations or black speckles. Discard any such areas.

Place the yuca, lime juice and salt in a pot and cover with about 2 inches (5 cm) of water. Bring to a boil over high heat. Lower the heat to a slow boil and cook, uncovered, for 25 to 30 minutes, or until the yuca is easily pierced with a fork.

When the yuca has about 5 minutes left to cook, pour the *mojo criollo* into a large skillet with the onion rings and heat to a gentle bubble to soften the onion.

Remove the cooked yuca from the water and pull out the fibrous stringy piece from each core.

Add the cooked yuca to the skillet and toss to combine with the sauce. Let the flavors mingle for 3 to 5 minutes, stirring a few times. The sauce will thicken during this time as some of the starch from the yuca cooks out. Serve as a starchy side to your favorite main dish. Leftovers will not reheat well; see the note as to how to use them.

NOTE: A tip for cooking leftover *yuca con mojo* is to form it into patties to fry. Mash the yuca and onion together and form into small balls, then flatten and fry in your fat of choice in a large skillet until crispy, 3 to 5 minutes per side.

AIP COMPLIANT: Use the AIP-compliant version of Mojo Criollo (page 154).

YUCA FRITA
YUCA FRIES

Pan-Latin

Yuca is an excellent replacement for white potatoes, especially as an alternative to french fries. French fries can take forever to cook if you are pan frying them, but these are ready much quicker. You can make *yuca frita* from either the fresh root or frozen chunks. I always prefer to work with frozen whenever possible (see page 174 for more info about using yuca), but in this case it is a bit easier to work with the fresh root. The trick to perfectly crispy on the outside yet tender on the inside yuca fries is to cut them to the right thickness and not boil them for too long before frying.

SERVES 2 TO 4

1 to 2 lb (455 to 905 g) fresh or frozen yuca

About ¼ cup (56 g) fat for frying (avocado oil or lard recommended)

Fine Himalayan salt

Chopped fresh cilantro, for garnish (optional)

If you are using fresh yuca, remove the peel with a sharp knife or vegetable peeler. Ensure that you remove all of the pink/purple layer beneath the tough outer peel. Cut the root crosswise into lengths of about 3 inches (7.5 cm). Cut each in half lengthwise and cut out the woody stem in the center of the root. Cut each piece into sticks about ¾-inch (2-cm) thick. Inspect the flesh to ensure it is pure white with no soft spots, discolorations or black speckles. Discard any such areas.

If you are using frozen yuca, add the pieces to a pot and cover with water. Bring to a boil, then lower the heat to a simmer and cook for several minutes, until thawed enough to cut. Drain and cut as described for fresh yuca.

Place the yuca sticks in a pot and cover with water. Bring to a boil over high heat, then lower the heat to a low boil and cook them for 10 to 15 minutes. They should be tender when pierced with a fork, but not falling apart. Drain the water and either fry the yuca sticks immediately or store them, covered, in the fridge to fry later or the following day.

In a small to medium skillet, heat your fat of choice over medium heat for 3 to 4 minutes. Add the yuca sticks and fry them for 2 to 3 minutes per side, or until they are lightly golden brown and crisp on the outside. Use additional fat as needed.

Sprinkle with salt to taste and garnish with chopped cilantro. Enjoy alone or dipped in Salsa de Ajo or Salsa Rosada (page 157) or another sauce from the "Los Esenciales" chapter.

AIP COMPLIANT: No adjustments necessary!

COUVE À MINEIRA
BRAZILIAN GARLICKY COLLARD GREENS

 Brazil

There isn't a whole lot of greenery in traditional Latin American cuisine, so I had to be sure to include this delicious recipe for collard greens that is a common side dish in Brazil. You can substitute your favorite variety of kale, if you prefer. It is such a simple cooking method but really makes the greens taste wonderful!

SERVES 2 TO 4

1 bunch collard greens (7 or 8 leaves)

2 tbsp (30 ml) extra-virgin olive oil

4 to 6 cloves garlic

¼ tsp fine Himalayan salt

Prepare the collard leaves by cutting away the thick stem. Lay each leaf flat on your cutting board, slice out the stem with a V shape, then cut the leaf in half by slicing above the V-shaped cut.

Place about 6 leaf halves in a stack and roll them up tightly to do a chiffonade cut. Slice thin strips (½ inch [1.3 cm] or less) crosswise, then carefully do one lengthwise cut through the center so that you are left with short ribbons of collards. Repeat until all leaves are cut into ribbons.

In a large skillet, heat the olive oil over medium heat for about 1 minute. Add the garlic and salt and sauté until the garlic is nice and fragrant, 1 to 2 minutes. Stir in the collard ribbons and sauté them, stirring frequently, until they are softened and bright green in color, 4 to 8 minutes. If they begin to turn dark, they are overcooking and may be bitter. Serve fresh with your favorite main dish.

AIP COMPLIANT: No adjustments necessary!

"CARAOTAS" NEGRAS DE VEGETALES
VEGETABLE BLACK "BEANS"

Venezuela

This is a lower-carb vegetable-based bean replacement that you can enjoy as a part of the dish Pabellón Criollo (page 47) or as a side with another dish of your choosing. You may also use it as a filling for Pupusas con Chicharrón o "Queso" (page 63). It is seasoned in the style of Venezuelan black beans, called *caraotas negras*. Using eggplant yields a firmer texture than zucchini, but both taste great. See page 129 for an alternative recipe that is starchy and has a more robust texture.

SERVES 4 TO 6

8 oz (225 g) bacon

1½ lb (680 g) zucchini, sliced, or eggplant, cubed

1 small onion, diced

1 small red bell pepper, diced

1 tbsp (7 g) cumin

1½ tsp (3 g) dried oregano

1 tbsp (15 ml) molasses

1 tbsp (15 ml) balsamic vinegar or freshly squeezed lime juice

2 tbsp (16 g) tapioca starch

2 tbsp (30 ml) water or Chicken Broth (page 168)

Fine Himalayan salt, to taste

In a large skillet, cook the bacon over medium heat until it is crispy, 8 to 12 minutes depending on the thickness. Transfer to a paper towel–lined plate, leaving the bacon fat in the skillet.

Cook the zucchini or eggplant in the rendered bacon fat. You may need to add additional fat if using eggplant, because it really soaks it up. Cook until tender, 8 to 10 minutes for zucchini and 10 to 15 minutes for eggplant.

Add the onion, pepper, cumin, oregano, molasses and vinegar to the pan and cook for about 5 more minutes. In a small bowl, create a slurry of the tapioca starch and water (or broth), pour it into the pan and cook for 2 minutes more.

Transfer the contents of the pan and the crispy bacon to a food processor or blender and blend until smooth. Season with salt to taste.

AIP COMPLIANT: This recipe can be used as an AIP reintroduction recipe for the spice cumin. Simply omit the red pepper and use zucchini instead of eggplant to make it nightshade-free.

"CARAOTAS" NEGRAS DE YUCA
YUCA BLACK "BEANS"

Venezuela

Of all the non-Paleo foods to create a Paleo-friendly replacement for, beans were the hardest to replicate. This dish has the authentic flavor of the Venezuelan black bean dish *caraotas negras*. I think that the base of yuca to replace the beans helps recreate some of the same texture as eating real beans, but of course it won't fool anyone into thinking they are eating actual beans. *Caraotas negras* are one of the four components of what is considered the national dish of Venezuela: Pabellón Criollo (page 47). You may also use it as a filling for Pupusas con Chicharrón o "Queso" (page 63). If you prefer a lower-carb option, see page 127 for an alternative recipe.

SERVES 4 TO 6

6 oz (170 g) bacon

11 oz (310 g) peeled yuca

8 oz (225 g) white or baby portobello mushrooms

1 small onion, diced

1 small red pepper, diced

2 cups (475 ml) Chicken Broth (page 168)

1 tbsp (15 ml) molasses

1 tbsp (15 ml) balsamic vinegar or freshly squeezed lime juice

1 tbsp (7 g) ground cumin

Fine Himalayan salt, to taste

In a large skillet, cook the bacon over medium heat until it is crispy, 8 to 12 minutes depending on the thickness. Transfer to a paper towel–lined plate, leaving the bacon fat in the skillet.

Meanwhile, coarsely "rice" the peeled yuca using a food processor. Cut it into several smaller chunks, then pulse 10 to 20 times. Do not overprocess. Set aside in a bowl and wipe out the food processor bowl.

Fry the mushrooms, onion and red pepper in the rendered bacon fat until softened, about 5 minutes, then remove with a slotted spoon. Coarsely process the mushroom mixture with the crispy bacon in the food processor. Do not overprocess; you want the mixture to be slightly chunky.

Add the yuca and broth to the skillet and cook, stirring frequently, for 15 minutes, or until very thick. Return the mushroom mixture to the pan along with the rest of the ingredients, including salt to taste, and mix well. Cook for about 5 minutes longer.

AIP COMPLIANT: This recipe can be used as an AIP reintroduction recipe for the spice cumin. Simply omit the red pepper to make it nightshade-free.

UN POCO DULCE

A LITTLE SWEET

Every great meal deserves something a little sweet to round out the dining experience. In this chapter you will find an enticing variety of traditional desserts to please your palate without making you feel like you have a sugar overload.

FLAN DE COCO
COCONUT MILK CUSTARD

 Puerto Rico

Flan is a custard with a caramel sauce that is popular throughout Latin America. *Flan de coco* is made with coconut milk, but is usually mixed with whole milk or condensed milk. Luckily, it tastes just as rich and wonderful when made with all coconut milk—including condensed coconut milk, which you can make at home or purchase in cans.

MAKES 2 (5-INCH [12.5-CM]) MINI FLANS TO SERVE 4 TO 6

½ cup (115 g) coconut sugar or grated *panela*

4 large eggs

1 (13.5-oz [399-ml]) can full-fat coconut milk

1 cup (235 ml) condensed coconut milk (purchased or make your own; see note page 135)

1 tbsp (15 ml) vanilla extract

Preheat the oven to 350°F (180°C).

Make the caramel sauce by combining the sugar with 2 tablespoons (30 ml) of water in a saucepan and heating over medium heat. Cook until slightly thickened, swirling occasionally to dissolve the sugar, 6 to 8 minutes.

Meanwhile, thoroughly blend the eggs, coconut milks and vanilla, either using a whisk or electric mixer or blender.

Pour the caramel sauce into the bottom of two 5-inch (12.5-cm) pie dishes, carefully tilting to swirl it along the sides. Allow to rest for about 5 minutes.

Divide the egg mixture evenly among your dishes.

Prepare a hot water bath by boiling water. Place your dishes in the bottom of an 9 x 13-inch (23 x 33-cm) ovenproof glass dish (or equivalent pan) and pour in enough hot water so that it comes about 1 inch (2.5 cm) up the sides of the dish. Take care not to get water in the flan itself and not to splash hot water while transferring the dish to the oven.

Bake for about 1 hour, or until a knife comes out clean when inserted into the center of a flan and the middle no longer wiggles if you shake the pan (remove from the water bath before testing for wiggles!). Wear sturdy ovenproof mitts to lift them from the water bath, or slip a cooking spatula (the kind you would flip pancakes with) underneath to lift. Be very careful not to burn yourself!

Allow the flan to cool for at least 20 minutes before refrigerating. Cover with plastic wrap and let chill for several hours before serving.

Release the flans onto a serving plate (make sure it has a lip to catch the sauce) by using a butter knife to gently loosen the edges. Place the plate on top of the dish and quickly flip it over to release onto the plate. The caramel sauce will drizzle out on top.

Serve each slice with a generous spoonful of caramel.

NOTE: You will need a large baking dish or roasting pan to make the hot water bath. Ensure that your mini pie dishes are small enough to fit inside the vessel you will use for your water bath. Two 5-inch (12.5-cm) mini pie pans fit perfectly inside of a 9 x 13-inch (23 x 33-cm) glass baking dish.

AIP COMPLIANT: Eggs are crucial to flan, so if you are AIP you can treat this dish as a reintroduction test for eggs.

PASTEL DE TRES "LECHES"
CAKE SOAKED IN 3 "MILKS"

Pan-Latin

Tres leches means "three milks" and in the traditional version this would be a blend of heavy cream, evaporated milk and sweetened condensed milk. Luckily, this dessert can be made dairy-free thanks to our friend the coconut. This cake is delicious any time you get a hankering for it, but since it is served chilled, it is especially refreshing in the summer months.

SERVES 9 TO 12

FOR THE CAKE
1 cup (112 g) sifted coconut flour

2 tbsp (16 g) tapioca starch, plus more for dusting the pan

1 tbsp (14 g) unflavored gelatin

2 tsp (8 g) baking soda

¼ tsp fine Himalayan salt

½ cup (120 ml) melted coconut oil, plus more for greasing the pan

⅔ cup (120 g) coconut sugar or grated *panela*

2 large eggs, or ½ cup (125 g) applesauce

½ tsp vanilla extract

1 tsp (5 ml) apple cider vinegar

⅔ cup (157 ml) water

FOR THE THREE MILKS
½ cup (120 ml) coconut cream

½ cup (120 ml) coconut milk

½ cup (120 ml) sweetened condensed coconut milk (purchased or make your own; see note)

Preheat the oven to 350°F (180°C).

To prepare the cake, in a mixing bowl, combine the coconut flour, tapioca starch, gelatin, baking soda and salt and stir well.

In a separate mixing bowl, combine the coconut oil, sugar, egg, vanilla and vinegar and whisk vigorously or beat with an electric mixer. Stir in the water.

Gradually add the dry ingredients to the wet, stirring often, until all ingredients are combined. The resulting batter will be extremely thick.

Grease an 8-inch (20.5-cm) square baking dish with coconut oil and dust lightly with tapioca starch. Use a spatula to scrape the batter into the dish, spreading it evenly so that there are no air bubbles in the batter and smoothing the top. Bake for 30 to 40 minutes, or until the edges have begun to pull away from the sides and the top is lightly crisped and has darkened. Due to the combination of coconut flour and coconut sugar, the cake does not turn a golden color. Be careful not to burn the cake. Allow it to remain in the dish while you prepare the milks.

Prepare the three milks: In a bowl, thoroughly combine the coconut cream, coconut milk and sweetened condensed coconut milk.

Transfer the cake to a serving platter by placing it on top of the pan and quickly inverting it. Or, if your baking dish has a lid, you may leave it there if you prefer. Use a fork or toothpick to prick holes all over the top of the cake. Pour the three-milk mixture on top in an even layer. Cover and chill in the refrigerator for at least 1 hour before serving.

NOTE: To make condensed coconut milk, place 1 cup (235 ml) of coconut milk in a saucepan and bring to a boil, stirring constantly to prevent bubbling over. Immediately lower the heat to low and stir in 2 to 4 tablespoons (30 to 45 g) of your sweetener of choice. Allow to simmer, stirring occasionally, until reduced by half (you should have ½ cup [120 ml]), 30 to 40 minutes.

AIP COMPLIANT: Use applesauce instead of egg.

TEMBLEQUE
COCONUT MILK PUDDING

Puerto Rico

The word *tembleque* means "wiggly" or "wobbly" and it is the perfect name for this creamy pudding. This dish is naturally dairy-free, thanks to the coconut milk base, although it is traditionally made with cornstarch as the thickener. For a lower-carb, Paleo-friendly option, gelatin works wonderfully to set this pudding. Other starches do not produce the pudding-like texture that cornstarch does, and in fact, tests using tapioca starch were what led to my developing the cheese recipe on page 170!

SERVES 6 TO 8

2 tbsp (28 g) unflavored gelatin

2 (13.5-oz [399-ml]) cans coconut milk

5 to 6 tbsp (100 to 120 g) honey, coconut sugar or grated *panela*

Pinch of fine Himalayan salt

Ground cinnamon, for garnish

Bloom the gelatin by pouring ½ cup (120 ml) of water into the bottom of a small saucepan and then sprinkling the gelatin slowly on top of the water. Do not add the gelatin too quickly or clumps can form. Whisk the mixture to encourage wetting, if needed.

Add the remaining ingredients, except the cinnamon, to the saucepan and heat over medium heat, whisking frequently, until all the gelatin and your choice of sweetener have dissolved.

Pour into a 9-inch (23-cm)-diameter x 1¼-inch (3-cm)-deep pie mold and allow to set for several hours in the refrigerator until firm. Serve in slices, almost like a crustless cheesecake for a traditional presentation. You can also pour the mixture into 6 to 8 small bowls, ramekins or other vessels. Sprinkle a generous amount of cinnamon on top before serving chilled.

AIP COMPLIANT: No adjustments necessary!

"ARROZ" CON DULCE
"RICE" PUDDING

 Puerto Rico

Arroz con dulce is a very typical dessert served throughout Latin America. This version is done in the style of Puerto Rico. It turns out that in this case, yuca makes the absolute perfect grain-free rice replacement. As it simmers in the coconut milk, it naturally thickens to a pudding-like consistency, thanks to the starch cooking out of the yuca. This stuff tastes like the real deal!

SERVES 4

About 5 oz (140 g) yuca

2 cups (475 ml) coconut milk

1 tsp (2 g) ground cinnamon, plus more for garnish

½ tsp ground ginger

¼ tsp ground cloves

5 to 6 tbsp (75 to 90 g) coconut sugar or grated *panela*

¼ cup (35 g) raisins

If using fresh yuca, peel the root with a knife or sharp vegetable peeler, ensuring you remove all traces of the pink/purple layer just beneath the skin. Cut off both tips and cut the root crosswise into sections about 3 inches (7.5 cm) long. Cut each in half lengthwise and cut out the woody stem in the center of the root. Inspect the flesh to ensure it is pure white with no soft spots, discolorations or black speckles. Discard any such areas.

If using frozen yuca, remove any remnants of the woody core.

Place the yuca in a food processor and pulse, using the blade attachment, to "rice" the yuca. Do not overprocess.

Place all the ingredients, except the raisins, in a pot and bring to a simmer over medium heat. Simmer for about 15 minutes, stirring constantly, until it is very thick and the yuca pieces are tender. Fold in the raisins and transfer to a serving dish. Place in the refrigerator to chill before serving. Garnish with cinnamon before serving.

> **AIP COMPLIANT:** No adjustments necessary!

HOJALDRE
PUERTO RICAN SPICE CAKE

Puerto Rico

Hojaldre is a delightful Puerto Rican spice cake. These flavors just scream "holidays" and I'm sure you'll love to make it. This base cake recipe is one of my specialties and borrows a note from traditional baking in my home state of Georgia by adding gelatin to the dry ingredients. This ensures an incredibly moist cake, whereas Paleo cakes generally tend to be on the dry side. Also, if you opt to use applesauce instead of the egg, the cake will be even moister! Traditional recipes call for a sweet wine, but you can also use plain grape juice.

SERVES ABOUT 16

FOR THE CAKE

2 cups (224 g) sifted coconut flour

4 tbsp (32 g) tapioca starch, plus more for dusting the pan

2 tbsp (28 g) unflavored gelatin

4 tsp (16 g) baking soda

½ tsp fine Himalayan salt

2 tsp (3 g) ground cinnamon

2 tsp (4 g) ground nutmeg or mace

1 tsp (2 g) ground cloves

1 cup (235 ml) melted coconut oil or palm shortening, plus more for pan

1½ to 1¾ cups (338 to 294 g) coconut sugar or grated *panela*

4 large eggs, or 1 cup (245 g) applesauce

1 tsp (5 ml) vanilla extract

2 tsp raw (10 ml) apple cider vinegar

⅔ cup (160 ml) sweet wine (Moscato works well)

⅔ cup (157 ml) water

FOR THE POWDERED SUGAR

¼ cup (60 g) coconut sugar or *panela* (or other unrefined granulated sweetener)

1½ tsp (12 g) tapioca starch

To prepare the cake, preheat the oven to 350°F (180°C).

In a mixing bowl, combine the coconut flour, tapioca starch, gelatin, baking soda, salt and spices and stir well. In a separate mixing bowl, combine the coconut oil, sugar, eggs, vanilla and vinegar and whisk vigorously or beat with an electric mixer. Stir in the wine and water. Gradually add the dry ingredients to the wet, stirring often, until all the ingredients are combined. The resulting batter will be extremely thick and almost doughlike, but the resulting cake will be very moist, so don't be alarmed.

Grease a 9-inch (23-cm) diameter x 3-inch (4.5-cm) deep fluted Bundt pan and dust lightly with tapioca starch. Use a spatula to scrape the batter into the pan, pressing it down and spreading it evenly so that there are no air bubbles in the batter.

Bake for 50 to 60 minutes, or until the top is lightly crisped and has darkened. A toothpick inserted into the center will come out mostly clean—however, due to the moist nature of this cake, some crumbs may still stick even when the cake is cooked through. Also, due to the combination of coconut flour and coconut sugar, the cake does not turn a golden color, and instead darkens slightly. Be careful not to burn the cake. Allow to cool in the pan for at least 30 minutes, then transfer very carefully to a serving plate to finish cooling. The texture of this cake is too delicate for a wire rack.

Prepare the powdered sugar: In a coffee grinder or high-powered blender, pulverize the coconut sugar and tapioca starch together. If purchasing powdered sugar, be sure to read the ingredients to make sure it contains tapioca starch and not cornstarch. Dust the top of the cake with the powdered sugar and serve.

AIP COMPLIANT: Use mace instead of nutmeg, applesauce instead of egg and juice or water instead of wine

CAZUELA
PUMPKIN BONIATO CRUSTLESS PIE

 Puerto Rico

The word *cazuela* means "cooking pot" and in most parts of Latin America it is used to describe stewed meats with vegetables. However, in Puerto Rico *cazuela* is a crustless pumpkin and boniato pie that is traditionally dairy-free, thanks to the use of coconut milk. It is typically thickened with eggs, but since eggs and I don't get along very well, I developed this egg-free version that is just as delicious. If you wish to be very traditional, make this using boniato and calabaza squash, or for a shortcut, use canned pumpkin and substitute white sweet potatoes for the boniato.

SERVES 9 TO 12

1¾ cups (394 g) mashed boniato or white or yellow sweet potatoes (from about 1 lb [455 g] peeled and cubed root)

1¾ cups (394 g) mashed calabaza squash (from about 1 lb [455 g] peeled and seeded squash), or 1 (15-oz [425-g] can pumpkin puree)

1½ cups (355 ml) coconut milk

4 tbsp (60 g) unflavored gelatin

½ to ⅔ cup (115 to 150 g) coconut sugar

1 tsp (2 g) ground cinnamon

½ tsp ground ginger

½ tsp aniseeds

½ tsp ground cloves

¼ tsp fine Himalayan salt

Place the peeled and cubed boniato and calabaza in a pot and cover with water. Bring to a boil over high heat and cook until all the pieces are fork-tender, about 20 minutes. Drain, place in a mixing bowl and mash to a smooth consistency. If the boniato is particularly stringy, puree the mixture in a food processor or with an immersion blender until very smooth.

Pour the coconut milk in a small pot and gradually sprinkle the gelatin on top, whisking frequently to combine it. Do not allow clumps to form. Once all of the gelatin has been wetted, heat the pan over medium heat, whisking often, until all the gelatin dissolves smoothly.

Combine all the remaining ingredients with the boniato mixture and pour in the coconut milk mixture. You can add the sugar gradually and taste the batter until it is as sweet as you like. Pour the batter into an 8-inch (20.5-cm) square glass dish, cover and refrigerate for several hours until set. Serve chilled.

AIP COMPLIANT: Omit the aniseeds and optionally replace with ½ teaspoon of ground mace.

PANETELA DE GUAYABA
GUAVA-STUFFED CAKE

 Puerto Rico

Guayaba (a.k.a. guava) is a tropical fruit that is a favorite in desserts throughout Latin America. You can readily find guava paste in stores or order it online. This cake is soft and fluffy with a warm, gooey filling and oh so delicious!

SERVES 9 TO 12

1 cup (112 g) sifted coconut flour

2 tbsp (16 g) tapioca starch, plus more for dusting the pan

1 tbsp (14 g) gelatin

2 tsp (8 g) baking soda

¼ tsp fine Himalayan salt

½ cup (120 ml) coconut oil, plus more for greasing the pan

⅔ cup (120 g) coconut sugar or grated *panela*

2 eggs, or ½ cup (125 g) applesauce

½ tsp vanilla extract

1 tsp (5 ml) apple cider vinegar

⅔ cup (157 ml) water

⅔ cup (157 ml) coconut milk

10 to 12 oz (283 to 340 g) guava paste, cut into about 16 slices

Preheat the oven to 350°F (180°C).

In a mixing bowl, combine the coconut flour, tapioca starch, gelatin, baking soda and salt and stir well.

In a separate mixing bowl, combine the coconut oil, sugar, eggs, vanilla and vinegar and whisk vigorously or beat with an electric mixer. Stir in the water and coconut milk. Gradually add the dry ingredients to the wet, stirring often, until all the ingredients are combined. The resulting batter will be extremely thick.

Grease an 8-inch (20.5-cm) square baking dish with coconut oil and dust lightly with tapioca starch. Use a spatula to scrape half of the batter into the dish, spreading it evenly so that there are no air bubbles in the batter. Add a layer of guava paste slices to cover, then add the remaining batter on top of the guava paste, smoothing it out with the spatula.

Bake for 30 to 40 minutes, or until the top is lightly crisped and has darkened. Due to the combination of coconut flour and coconut sugar, the cake does not turn a golden color. Be careful not to burn the cake. Can be served hot while the filling is gooey (how I prefer it) or at room temperature.

AIP COMPLIANT: Use applesauce instead of egg. This actually results in a moister cake!

PLÁTANOS CALADOS
STEWED SPICED RIPE PLANTAINS

Colombia

Plantains are so extremely versatile and can be appropriate for breakfast, lunch, dinner and dessert! This recipe utilizes very ripe plantains that are mostly black and soft to the touch. They are naturally very sweet on their own and pair wonderfully with the warm spices. In the fall when everyone is going crazy for "pumpkin spice" everything, make a batch of these!

SERVES 2 TO 4

1 cup (235 ml) water

¼ cup (60 g) coconut sugar or grated *panela* sugar

1 tsp (2 g) ground cinnamon

½ tsp aniseeds

¼ tsp ground cloves

1 tbsp (15 ml) coconut oil

2 large, very ripe (mostly black) plantains, peeled and cut into 4 pieces

In a small pot, combine all the ingredients, except the plantains, and stir well. Add the plantains and bring to a boil, then lower the heat to medium, cover and cook for 15 to 20 minutes, or until the sauce thickens and the plantains are cooked throughout and tender.

Serve with a generous portion of sauce and enjoy!

AIP COMPLIANT: Omit the aniseeds and optionally replace with ½ teaspoon of ground mace.

LOS ESENCIALES

THE ESSENTIALS
(SAUCES, COOKING BASES
AND MORE)

In traditional Latin American cuisine, the flavorful cooking bases that you begin with
and the exotic condiments that adorn the table at mealtime are crucial components
of the food. The secret to elevating meals from delicious to simply divine lies in these
Latin kitchen essentials. Your taste buds will rejoice in the exciting layers of flavor that
the recipes in this chapter will lend to your eating experience.

Mojo Criollo, recipe on page 154.

SOFRITO
FLAVORFUL COOKING BASE

 Puerto Rico

Sofrito is the seasoning mixture that is the backbone of Puerto Rican cooking and is an important component of many recipes in this book. This delightful blend of herbs, peppers, spices and alliums packs a powerful and distinctive punch of flavor. I recommend making a batch and freezing it in 1 tablespoon (13 g) portions with an ice cube tray. That way you will have a steady supply for any recipe.

MAKES ABOUT 1½ CUPS (330 G)

1 cup (4 g) packed cilantro (lower stems removed)

½ cup (2 g) packed culantro (lower 3" to 4" [7.5 to 10 cm] of stems removed; if unavailable, use additional cilantro)

1 head garlic, separated into cloves and peeled

1 tbsp (6 g) minced fresh oregano, or 1 tsp (2 g) dried

½ to 1 tsp (3 to 6 g) fine Himalayan salt

2 red bell peppers, stemmed and seeded and cut into a few pieces

8 *ajíes dulces* (if unavailable, substitute 1 additional red bell pepper)

½ yellow onion

1 tbsp (15 ml) extra-virgin olive oil

Place all the ingredients in a blender or food processor and blend until smooth. Best when used within 1 to 2 days. Do not store in refrigerator for longer. Instead, freeze extra in ice cube trays, measuring 1 tablespoon (14 g) in each well of the tray. Once frozen, transfer to a large resealable plastic freezer bag and use within 3 months.

AIP COMPLIANT: Replace the peppers with a mixture of 1 cup (100 g) of chopped celery and 1 cup (130 g) of chopped carrot, making a sauce that allows you to create surprisingly authentic-tasting dishes without the nightshades.

ADOBO MOJADO
GARLIC OREGANO WET RUB

 Puerto Rico

Adobo is a misunderstood term that simply refers to any seasoning mixture used to flavor meat. It is typically a paste that uses a little oil to help it stick to the meat, hence "mojado," which means "wet." This version is very typical in the region of Puerto Rico where Milagros is from. Don't be intimidated by the amount of garlic. Other regions use different ratios and in other countries in Latin America different seasonings are used. The *adobo mojado* is what makes Milagros's pork roast (page 16) so "famous"! But you can use this blend on a wide range of meats to create a wonderfully flavorful meal.

ENOUGH FOR 4 TO 5 LB (1.8 TO 2.3 KG) OF MEAT

2 tbsp (20 g) minced garlic (about 1 whole head)

1½ tsp (9 g) fine Himalayan salt

1½ tsp (3 g) dried oregano

1 tsp (2 g) freshly ground black pepper

½ tsp ground turmeric

1 tsp (2 g) ground coriander seeds

1½ tbsp (23 ml) extra-virgin olive oil

1½ tbsp (23 ml) freshly squeezed lime juice

In a bowl, combine all the ingredients, scaling the amounts up or down depending on how large your piece of meat is. Rub generously on the meat you wish to season. Use it to season a whole chicken or turkey, pork roasts (see page 16), pork ribs or chops, beef roasts, even steaks. Marinate meats in airtight containers in the fridge for up to 24 hours in this adobo for easy, flavorful meals.

AIP COMPLIANT: Simply omit the black pepper and coriander seeds. The flavors are still perfectly balanced for delicious results.

AJILIMÓJILI SAUCE
GARLIC PEPPER SAUCE

Puerto Rico

This sauce with a funny name (pronounced: ah-*hee*-lee-MOH-hee-lee) packs a lot of sweet, garlic-forward flavor and is a delightful accompaniment to grilled or roasted meats or with many of the various fritters in the "¡Comida de Fiesta!" chapter.

MAKES ABOUT 1¼ CUPS (285 ML)

1 tbsp (10 g) peeled and minced garlic

3 tbsp (3 g) finely chopped culantro (may substitute cilantro)

6 *ajíes dulces,* or 1 small red bell pepper, stemmed, seeded and minced

½ tsp freshly ground black pepper

1 tsp (6 g) fine Himalayan salt

½ cup (120 ml) extra-virgin olive oil

1 tbsp (15 ml) coconut vinegar

1 tbsp (15 ml) freshly squeezed lime juice

In a bowl, combine all the ingredients and whisk well. Or place everything in a food processor or blender and puree into a smooth sauce. Cover and place in the refrigerator for 30 to 60 minutes to allow the flavors to combine before serving. Serve as a sauce for Tostones (page 115) or use it as a marinade or cooking sauce for a variety of meats or seafood.

AIP COMPLIANT: Omit the ajíes dulces or bell peppers and replace with 2 medium carrots, cut into a few pieces.

MOJO DE AJO
GARLIC-OLIVE OIL SAUCE

 Puerto Rico

Mojo de ajo is essentially a chunky garlic-infused oil that pairs perfectly with Tostones (page 115), Yuca Frita (page 124), many of the other fritters in the "¡Comida de Fiesta!" chapter or even with steak or simple roasted chicken. Note that sometimes due to a normal chemical reaction between the garlic and the acid of the lime juice, the garlic may turn a blue-green color as it cooks. This is harmless, but can make for interesting conversation.

MAKES ABOUT ¼ CUP (60 ML)

¼ cup (60 ml) extra-virgin olive oil

1 tsp (3 g) minced garlic

Juice of ¼ lime

¼ tsp fine Himalayan salt

Place all the ingredients in a small saucepan and simmer over low heat for about 10 minutes. The olive oil should bubble gently but do not brown (overcook) the garlic.

Store in the fridge in an airtight container for up to 3 days.

AIP COMPLIANT: No changes needed!

MOJO CRIOLLO

SOUR ORANGE MARINADE

 Cuba

Sour oranges are a wonderful seasoning agent in Cuban and Puerto Rican cuisine. The flavor is actually more bitter than sour and works well to impart a tangy flavor to everything from roasts to veggies to starchy sides. You can make a large portion and freeze it for later use, too. If sour oranges are unavailable in your area, I've given you two substitutions using more commonly available citrus fruits that you can try out.

MAKES ABOUT 1½ CUPS (355 ML)

1 cup (240 ml) freshly squeezed sour orange juice

8 to 10 cloves garlic, peeled

1 tsp (2 g) dried oregano

1 tsp (6 g) fine Himalayan salt

¼ tsp freshly ground black pepper

2 to 4 tbsp (30 to 60 ml) extra-virgin olive oil, depending on recipe

In a blender or food processor, pulse the sour orange juice, garlic, oregano, salt, pepper and olive oil until the garlic is pulverized and you have a sauce with a creamy consistency.

Use immediately as a marinade. Store in fridge for a few days only. Freeze unused portions for use later.

Used as a traditional marinade for meats (especially pork; see pages 40, 41 and 88), for yuca (page 154), served as a condiment for cooked meats or to season roasted or sautéed veggies. It is a very versatile marinade/dressing.

NOTE: Sour oranges are also called bitter, Seville, marmalade or bigarade oranges and may be labeled *"naranja agria"* at Latin American markets. If sour oranges are unavailable, substitute ½ cup (120 ml) of freshly squeezed lime juice and ½ cup (120 ml) of freshly squeezed regular (sweet) orange juice. Or use ½ cup (120 ml) of freshly squeezed regular orange juice, ¼ cup (60 ml) of grapefruit juice and 1 tablespoon (15 ml) of lime juice.

AIP COMPLIANT: Omit the ground black pepper

SALSA DE AJO Y SALSA ROSADA
GARLIC CILANTRO MAYONNAISE AND PINK SAUCE

Pan-Latin

There is nothing quite like the rich creaminess of freshly prepared mayonnaise at home. I have found that using a food processor results in perfect results every time. It is rare that you will find a plain mayonnaise accompanying Latin American meals, and instead you will find something like *salsa de ajo*. Use the plain mayonnaise with a Paleo-friendly ketchup to create one of the most popular condiments called *salsa rosada* (pink sauce).

MAKES ABOUT 1 CUP (225 G)

FOR PLAIN MAYONNAISE

1 large egg, at room temperature

¼ tsp fine Himalayan salt

1 cup (235 ml) avocado oil (recommended) or extra-virgin olive oil

1 tbsp (15 ml) freshly squeezed lime juice

FOR *SALSA DE AJO*

1 batch plain mayonnaise

½ cup (2 g) minced fresh cilantro

3 to 5 small cloves garlic, peeled

FOR *SALSA ROSADA*

½ cup (115 g) mayonnaise

¼ cup (60 g) ketchup

1½ tsp (8 ml) freshly squeezed lime juice

Dash of hot sauce (optional)

For plain mayonnaise, in a food processor, pulse the egg and salt to blend. With the motor running, pour in the oil in a thin stream. (Some food processors have a small hole in the feed tube specifically designed for making mayonnaise. Pour the oil into the tube and it will drip slowly, repeat until all oil has been added.) Add the lime juice and pulse to combine. Taste and add extra salt, if necessary.

For *salsa de ajo*, in a food processor, puree all the sauce ingredients until creamy. Taste and add extra salt, if necessary. Adjust the garlic level to your preferred taste.

For *salsa rosada*, place all the sauce ingredients in a bowl and stir to combine evenly. This goes especially well with Tostones (page 115), Yuca Fries (page 124) or on a Patacón Maracucho (page 72).

NOTE: This recipe contains raw eggs. Use fresh eggs with clean shells and do not allow contact between the yolk or white and the shell. You can now purchase pasteurized eggs at many grocery stores, if you would like to eliminate the concern of salmonella or other food-borne illness. Also, studies have shown that eggs from pasture-raised birds are extremely unlikely to be contaminated with salmonella, so if local farmers are raising birds on pasture, talk to them about their eggs. I buy mine from a farmer who uses his own eggs to make his own mayonnaise.

AIP COMPLIANT: For egg-free salsa de ajo, blend together 1 (14.1-oz [400-g]) can plain hearts of palm (drained), with 2 to 3 cloves peeled garlic, ½ cup (12 g) minced cilantro, 2 to 3 tablespoons (30 to 45 ml) lime juice and ½ to 1 teaspoon (2 to 5 g) fine Himalayan salt until a smooth puree forms. Some chefs in Central America make seasoned palm purees like this to accompany food and it makes a wonderful egg-free "mayo"!

CHIMICHURRI

GARLIC PARSLEY STEAK SAUCE

Argentina

Chimichurri is the traditional condiment for Churrasco (page 105), but it pairs well with any kind of steak, pork chops, grilled chicken and also flaky white fish. There is a misconception that this is a cilantro-based sauce; rather, flat-leaf parsley is the main ingredient. This recipe is made in the style of my favorite Argentinean steakhouse in Miami Beach. Even if you do not like parsley, you will enjoy the robust flavor of this *chimichurri*!

MAKES ABOUT 1 CUP (235 ML)

1 cup (60 g) fresh flat-leaf parsley, stemmed and finely chopped (ideally with a knife)

1 tbsp (5 g) dried oregano

1 tbsp (10 g) minced garlic (from about 1 small head)

1 tsp (6 g) fine Himalayan salt, or to taste

½ tsp freshly ground black pepper

½ cup (120 ml) extra-virgin olive oil

2 tbsp (30 ml) red wine vinegar or coconut vinegar

1 tbsp (15 ml) freshly squeezed lime juice

½ to 1 tsp (0.6 to 1.2 g) red pepper flakes (optional)

In a bowl with a lid, combine all the ingredients. Alternatively, use a food processor to combine, taking care to pulse only a few times to keep a coarse texture. Best served after allowing the flavors to meld for 30 to 60 minutes in the refrigerator. Store in an airtight container in the refrigerator for up to about 5 days.

AIP COMPLIANT: Omit the ground black pepper and do not include the optional red pepper flakes.

AJÍ PICANTE
SPICY GREEN ONION SAUCE

Colombia

If you have ever dined at a Colombian restaurant, you've likely seen a bowl of *ají picante* on every table to accompany pretty much every main dish. It features chunky green onions in a thin, tangy base and is meant to be spooned on top of arepas (pages 67 and 68), Carimañolas (page 71), steak, roasted chicken or even Tostones (page 115).

MAKES ABOUT 1 CUP (260 G)

½ cup (50 g) chopped green onions, including a few inches (cm) of the green part (about 1 bunch)

½ cup (8 g) minced cilantro (about 1 bunch, lower stems removed)

½ tsp fine Himalayan salt

1 tbsp (15 ml) extra-virgin olive oil

2 tbsp (30 ml) distilled white vinegar or coconut vinegar

2 tbsp (30 ml) freshly squeezed lime juice (from 1 to 2 limes)

6 tbsp (90 ml) filtered water

2 tbsp (23 g) minced tomato

½ minced jalapeño or habanero pepper, or to taste (omit if a mild sauce is desired)

In a nonreactive bowl, combine all the ingredients and stir well. Allow to sit for 10 to 15 minutes before serving, to allow the liquid to absorb the flavors of the ingredients. Store in an airtight container in the fridge for up to 3 to 5 days.

AIP COMPLIANT: Omit the tomato and hot peppers—the sauce is still extremely flavorful without the nightshades!

CURTIDO
SPICY CABBAGE SLAW

El Salvador

Curtido is a wonderfully delicious no-mayonnaise coleslaw that traditionally accompanies Pupusas con Chicharrón o "Queso" (page 63), but pairs well with fried eggs, steak, any type of roast, chicken or even Tostones (page 115). This is one of my favorite all-purpose condiments that I will sometimes eat more as a side dish than a condiment. It is certainly a delicious way to get more cabbage into your diet!

SERVES 4 TO 6

1 small head green cabbage, sliced very thinly or grated

4 carrots, grated

1 medium onion, thinly sliced and cut about 1" (2.5 cm) long

2 fresh jalapeño peppers, diced and seeded, or 1 to 2 cloves garlic, minced

2 tsp (12 g) fine Himalayan salt

2 tsp (4 g) dried oregano

½ cup (120 ml) filtered water

½ cup (120 ml) apple cider vinegar

In a large, nonreactive bowl, combine all the ingredients and stir well. Depending on how large your cabbage is, you may need to add a bit more vinegar and water. Place it in the fridge for 15 minutes before serving. The flavors will continue to develop as it sits. Serve a generous portion alongside Pupusas con Chicharrón o "Queso" (page 63).

Store in an airtight container in the fridge for up to 3 to 4 days.

AIP COMPLIANT: Simply omit the jalapeño peppers and substitute minced garlic.

SALSA VERDE MÁGICA
MAGIC GREEN SAUCE

 *Peru, Venezuela & Colombia*

I don't have a proper name for this sauce, but it is something I developed in my own kitchen after dining at numerous Peruvian, Venezuelan and Colombian restaurants and being served some sort of magical, delicious green sauce that prompted me to ask, "What is in this?" only to be told, with a grin, that it is a secret. This sauce goes great with just about everything—seriously.

MAKES ABOUT 1½ CUPS (355 ML)

2 bunches cilantro, lower stems removed (about 2 cups [32 g] packed)

3 to 6 cloves garlic

¼ cup (60 g) mayonnaise (page 157)

Juice of 2 limes

1 tsp (6 g) fine Himalayan salt

4 tbsp (60 ml) extra-virgin olive oil

1 serrano or jalapeño pepper, stemmed and seeded, or 1 tbsp (16 ml) Peruvian *ají amarillo* paste (optional)

¼ to ½ Hass avocado (optional, for a thicker sauce)

In a food processor, purée all the ingredients into a smooth paste. For a thicker sauce, add ¼ to ½ avocado. For best flavor and texture, refrigerate for at least 2 hours before serving. The sauce will thicken as it chills. Also, to change things up you can use half cilantro and half flat-leaf parsley.

AIP COMPLIANT: Omit the pepper and the mayonnaise and replace with ½ or 1 Hass avocado, adjusted to your preferred level of creaminess.

GUASACACA
SPICY AVOCADO SAUCE

Venezuela

Guasacaca is an avocado-based sauce that is similar to guacamole and can be made either chunky or blended to be smooth, depending on your preference. I like to blend it into a smooth texture. Using a large Florida-type avocado makes a lighter, smoother texture, but you can also use Hass avocados.

MAKES ABOUT 2 CUPS (450 G)

½ cup (8 g) chopped fresh cilantro

½ cup (20 g) chopped fresh flat-leaf parsley

6 green onions, including a few inches (cm) of the green part

1 tbsp (10 g) minced garlic

2 tsp (12 g) fine Himalayan salt

½ tsp freshly ground black pepper

½ to 1 jalapeño pepper, stemmed and seeded

1 large Florida-type avocado, or 2 to 3 Hass avocados

Juice of 2 limes

¼ cup (60 ml) extra-virgin olive oil

6 *ajíes dulces,* or 1 large red bell pepper, stemmed and seeded

In a food processor or blender, puree all the ingredients into a smooth sauce. Serve with Tostones (page 115), as a condiment with arepas (page 67 or 68) or slathered on a Patacón Maracucho (page 72).

AIP COMPLIANT: Omit the black pepper and peppers for a flavorful avocado sauce.

POLLO DESMENUZADO SENCILLO
SIMPLE SHREDDED CHICKEN

Pan-Latin

One of my favorite tricks for quick and easy meals is to have a stash of precooked shredded chicken on hand in my freezer. It's easy to prepare shredded chicken on the stovetop, in a slow cooker or (my favorite) in a pressure cooker, such as the Instant Pot®.

MAKES ABOUT 4 CUPS (560 G)

4 large boneless, skinless chicken breasts (about 2 lb [905 g])

Chicken Broth (page 168) or water

Stovetop directions: Place the chicken breasts in a saucepan and cover with chicken broth or water. Bring to a boil over high heat, then lower the heat to a simmer. Cook until the meat is no longer pink in the center, 10 to 12 minutes. Skim off and discard any foam that forms on the water. Shred the meat with 2 forks and store in an airtight container in the refrigerator for up to 4 days or in the freezer up to 3 months.

Slow cooker directions: Place the chicken breasts and 1 cup (235 ml) of water or broth in the crock of a slow cooker and cook on low for 4 to 5 hours. Shred the meat with 2 forks and store in an airtight container in the refrigerator for up to 4 days or in the freezer up to 3 months.

Instant Pot® pressure cooker directions: Place the chicken breasts and 1½ cups (355 ml) of water or broth in the stainless-steel liner of the Instant Pot® and cook under high pressure for 15 minutes. You can quick release the pressure or allow it to depressurize naturally. Shred the meat with 2 forks and store in an airtight container in the refrigerator for up to 4 days or in the freezer up to 3 months.

AIP COMPLIANT: Use water or an AIP-compliant broth if using store-bought.

CALDO DE POLLO
CHICKEN BROTH

Pan-Latin

Making flavorful and healthy bone broth at home is so easy and much more economical than purchasing broth. A pot of broth is really like a blank canvas—you can change the vegetables and seasonings to give each batch of broth a different personality. This particular blend lends a Latin American flair to the broth, making it perfect for the recipes in this cookbook.

MAKES ABOUT 2 QUARTS (1.9 L)

3 tbsp (45 ml) extra-virgin olive oil, to sauté vegetables (optional)

2 onions, chopped coarsely

1 large red bell pepper, chopped coarsely

4 to 5 carrots, peeled and chopped coarsely

3 stalks celery, chopped coarsely

½ head garlic, cloves peeled and chopped coarsely

3 to 4 lb (1.4 to 1.8 kg) chicken bones, wings, backs, necks and/or carcasses

3 bay leaves

Several sprigs fresh thyme

3 culantro leaves or 6 cilantro sprigs

1 tsp (6 g) fine Himalayan salt

1 tbsp (5 g) whole black peppercorns (optional)

3 to 4 quarts (2.8 to 3.8 L) water

Optional first step: In a large stockpot, heat the olive oil for 3 to 4 minutes, then add the onions, bell pepper, carrots, celery and garlic. Cook the vegetables, stirring frequently, until lightly browned, about 10 minutes. Add about 1 cup (235 ml) of water and scrape up any browned bits from the bottom of the pot. This step will add some depth of flavor to the broth, but may be skipped if you are short on time.

Add the remaining ingredients, ensuring that you also add enough water to cover everything. Bring to a boil over high heat, then lower the heat to a simmer. Gently skim off and discard any scum that rises to the top. Cover and continue to simmer for 1½ to 2½ more hours. Strain with a fine-mesh sieve or a cheesecloth-lined colander. Extra broth can easily be frozen in a resealable plastic bag or in freezer-safe pint-size, wide-mouth canning jars (ensure that you leave enough head space in the top to account for expansion during freezing). You can also freeze it in 1-tablespoon (15-ml) portions in an ice cube tray (like the Sofrito, page 148), then put the cubes in a large resealable freezer bag.

AIP COMPLIANT: Omit the red bell pepper and peppercorns.

"QUESO" AMARILLO
YELLOW "CHEESE"

Pan-Latin

This dairy-free cheese is a good complement to the white cheese on page 170. This cheese is more reminiscent of a cheddar, and if you are very careful you can shred this cheese. It does not stand up to heat as well as the white cheese and should only be melted for two to three minutes max, if you choose to use it as a melted topping.

MAKES ABOUT 8.5 OZ (240 G)

½ cup (120 ml) coconut milk

2 to 3 tsp (8 to 12 g) nutritional yeast

1 tsp (5 ml) freshly squeezed lemon juice

⅛ to ¼ tsp granulated garlic

⅛ to ¼ tsp granulated onion

1 to 2 tsp (5 to 10 ml) red palm oil (for color)

¼ tsp ground turmeric (optional, for brighter color)

¼ tsp fine Himalayan salt

4 tbsp (32 g) tapioca starch

4 tbsp (60 ml) Chicken Broth (page 168), divided

1 tbsp (14 g) unflavored gelatin

In a small saucepan, whisk together the coconut milk, yeast, lemon juice, garlic and onion powders, red palm oil, turmeric and salt. In a separate bowl, stir the tapioca starch into 2 tablespoons (30 ml) of the chicken broth to create a slurry. Pour the slurry into the coconut milk mixture. (Making a slurry is important to prevent clumping.) Next, add the remaining 2 tablespoons (30 ml) of chicken broth to the same bowl and use it to "bloom" the gelatin by slowly sprinkling the gelatin on top and allowing it to soak up the liquid. Stir occasionally through the process. You will be left with a smooth gel. Scoop it up and add it to the coconut milk mixture in the saucepan.

Heat the mixture over medium heat, whisking frequently, until the gelatin dissolves. Continue to heat for 8 to 10 minutes total. You will notice that it begins to thicken, and at this point you should whisk continuously. The consistency will noticeably change quickly when it is ready, and as you whisk it will pull away from the bottom of the pan and become very thick. Remove from the heat and pour into a container with a lid. Place it in the fridge or freezer until it is set.

Cut it into slices to include in Patacón Maracucho (page 72) or stuff inside Pupusas con Chicharrón o "Queso" (page 63) instead of the meat filling.

AIP COMPLIANT: No changes necessary!

"QUESO" BLANCO
WHITE "CHEESE"

Pan-Latin

This dairy-free cheese was born out of a failed attempt at making Tembleque (page 136), which taught me that heating coconut milk with tapioca starch causes a very interesting reaction and creates something that has a stretchy, mozzarella cheese–like texture. Adding a little bit of nutritional yeast and some lemon juice yields a mild white cheese that is perfect to stuff inside Aborrajados de Plátano (page 64) or to slice and melt on top of Canoas de Plátanos Maduros (page 87) or Chayotes Rellenos (page 43). It is also the key to creating Paleo Pandebono (page 59). This cheese is sticky, but it melts beautifully since there is no gelatin in it.

MAKES ABOUT 9½ OUNCES (275 G)

¾ cup (175 ml) full-fat coconut milk

½ tsp fine Himalayan salt

1½ tsp (6 g) nutritional yeast flakes, or more if desired

1½ to 2 tsp (8 to 10 ml) lemon juice or apple cider vinegar

1½ tsp (20 g) lard or extra-virgin olive oil

4½ tbsp (36 g) tapioca starch dissolved in 4½ tbsp (68 ml) water

In a small saucepan, whisk together the coconut milk, salt, nutritional yeast, lemon juice and lard and heat over medium heat until the lard melts. Pour the tapioca starch slurry into the pan.

Continue to heat over medium heat, whisking frequently, until the mixture begins to thicken. Then whisk constantly and watch as it gets very thick and gooey, almost curdled. Continue to cook, whisking constantly, until you see it pulling away from the bottom and sides as you whisk and also sticking to itself, 5 to 7 minutes total. It will look like a big pot of melted cheese, as it should, once it is done cooking.

Transfer to a glass container with a lid. Use a spatula to help remove it from the pan. It is extremely sticky and may not pour easily. Allow it to cool in the refrigerator until set, about 2 hours.

Once set, this "cheese" behaves like a fresh mozzarella. You can slice it or break it into small chunks to use in other recipes.

NOTE: Including the lard results in a cheese with more depth and that hint of flavor to signal to your taste buds "animal product," which makes it taste all the more believable. This "cheese" stretches similarly to mozzarella when it is cooked, and it can withstand heating in the oven for 10 minutes until bubbling and gooey while maintaining its stretch.

AIP COMPLIANT: No changes necessary!

STOCKING THE LATIN AMERICAN PALEO KITCHEN

SPECIAL LATIN AMERICAN INGREDIENTS

Inside this cookbook you will see some ingredients that may be new to you, so I'd like to give you a quick overview of each ingredient.

TROPICAL STARCHES

The availability of the following tropical starches will vary depending on your location. Generally speaking, these ingredients are more easily available in larger cities. If you have any sort of international market catering either to those from Asia or from Latin America, you will likely be able to find some, if not all, of these starches. You can also ask the produce manager of your grocery store if he or she can possibly order any of these for you, too.

PLANTAINS (CALLED *PLÁTANOS*)

Plantains are a type of banana that can be eaten only after being cooked and which can be peeled only with a knife. They can be utilized at any stage of ripeness and are generally grouped into three categories: green (unripe), mostly yellow (ripe) and mostly black (very ripe). A gradient does exist between ripe and very ripe, and when a recipe calls for ripe plantains, it will usually specify mostly yellow or yellow with some black.

To keep green plantains from ripening too quickly, you can store them in the refrigerator. Usually this will make them more difficult to peel. The trick to remove the peel more easily is to cut 1 or 2 slits down the length of the plantain, chop it crosswise into 2 to 4 pieces, place the pieces in a bowl and cover with water. Dissolve about ½ to 1 teaspoon (3 to 6 g) of salt in the water and let them soak for 15 to 20 minutes. This will loosen the peel.

GREEN BANANAS (CALLED *GUINEITOS*)

Recipes that call for green bananas refer to bananas that are totally green and unripe and which may be labeled as "for cooking" rather than "for eating." Sometimes you will be able to find these at regular grocery stores—ask your produce manager. It is important to only use very green bananas in these recipes or else the texture of the final product will not turn out correctly.

Sometimes you can also find peeled and frozen green bananas, either cut into disks or ground into a dough alone or with another tropical starch, such as malanga. For both Alcapurrias (page 60) and Pasteles (page 33) you may be lucky enough to find green banana dough labeled for use in these recipes, which can be a nice shortcut.

YUCA

Yuca (pronounced "YOU-kuh"), also known as manioc or cassava, is an incredible tropical starch. It is a tuberous root with a thick, bark-like peel. When the whole root is dried and ground into a flour, it is called cassava flour. The extracted starch is called tapioca starch. They behave differently in recipes and have different uses.

The yuca root is unfortunately highly perishable once it is dug out of the ground, so for it to survive import to the United States, it is coated in a thick wax. Even still, you will often find some or all of the yuca root you buy at the store to be unsound once you cut into it at home. The flesh should be pure white with no black speckles or other discoloration and no soft spots, otherwise it should be discarded. There is no way to tell whether the yuca root at the store is sound without breaking open the root, and sometimes you will see people doing this to check the roots before buying!

The good news is that you can usually find peeled, frozen yuca at most stores that carry the fresh roots. I always have a stash of yuca in my freezer and rarely buy the fresh roots. The price per pound is almost always much cheaper when buying frozen yuca, too.

When cooking yuca, be aware that there is a woody, stringy core in the very center that must be removed. It is easily separated from the soft flesh after boiling. Sometimes it will already be removed from frozen yuca.

Please do not make the mistake of calling it yucca ("YUCK-uh") as that is a type of agave and completely unrelated to this delightful root. For those avoiding nightshades, yuca is an excellent potato substitute.

MALANGA (ALSO CALLED *YAUTÍA* OR *OCUMO*)

Malanga is an interesting starchy root (botanically speaking, a corm) with a rough, hairy skin and pure white or slightly pink flesh. It looks very much like a piece of yuca, but is typically shorter and is not coated in wax. The flavor is actually quite strong, earthy, deep and husky. Interestingly, the plant is a type of elephant ear. It is a staple in Puerto Rican cuisine, but if you have trouble sourcing it you can generally replace it with taro.

TARO

Taro has a rich culinary history across the globe and is thought to be one of the earliest plants cultivated by humans. Due to the high content of oxalic acid you may need to wear gloves when peeling these roots, because they can cause skin irritation. However, once cooked, taro is an easily digested starch option and another fabulous nightshade-free alternative to potatoes. The flavor is milder than that of malanga and has a nutty quality.

There is some confusion about malanga and taro, and some people say they are the same thing. They aren't. While they are in the same family (Araceae), malanga belongs to the genus *Xanthosoma* and taro belongs to the genus *Colocasia*. They are related and are both elephant ear plants, but definitely not the same thing.

The fact that some stores and vendors label taro as *malanga isleña* only adds to the confusion. But, you can easily tell malanga and taro apart when you see them. Taro is more bulb- or barrel-shaped, has a smoother, not hairy, and lighter-colored skin marked with rings and the flesh inside is speckled with tiny pinkish-purplish dots.

ÑAME

Ñame is the Spanish word for "yam." Here in the United States we have a really terrible habit of calling sweet potatoes, which are in the same family as the morning glory (Convolvulaceae), yams. Sweet potatoes are not the same thing as yams. Yams are much larger, have a dark gray or dark brown slightly hairy skin, white or yellow flesh and a unique sweet flavor. They belong to the family Dioscoreaceae.

When choosing yams, be sure to press firmly all over to check for any soft spots. After peeling and cutting into the roots, discard any discolored or soft areas. White-fleshed sweet potatoes can be used to substitute these yams in many cases.

BONIATO (ALSO CALLED *BATATA* OR *CAMOTE*)

These tubers, which are also known as a Cuban sweet potatoes, have reddish-brown skin with white flesh. The texture is drier, mealier, and the tuber is less sweet than the yellow-fleshed variety of sweet potato typically eaten in the United States. The flavor is unique with a slight nuttiness and actually can work well in both sweet or savory dishes.

CALABAZA SQUASH (WEST INDIAN PUMPKIN)

This is a type of tropical squash that you will usually find cut into chunks in the refrigerated section of your local Latin grocery store as well as available whole. They are wider than they are tall. If you can't find it, don't worry; substitute any other orange-fleshed squash, such as butternut or acorn or pie pumpkin. When purchasing for a recipe, count on buying 1 pound (455 g) of peel-on, seeds-in calabaza for every ½ pound (225 g) of cleaned calabaza needed for a recipe.

OTHER TROPICAL PRODUCE

AJÍ DULCES

These sweet dwarf peppers look very much like habanero peppers but are totally mild. You can typically find them at Latin or Asian grocery stores and they may be green, red or yellow. If you cannot find them, you can substitute regular bell peppers, but they are worth seeking out due to the unique flavor.

PERUVIAN CHILE PEPPERS–AJÍ PANCA AND AJÍ AMARILLO

Ají panca are red and have a delightfully rich smoky flavor with very little heat. *Ají amarillo* peppers are quite hot and have a very bright, fresh, clean flavor. I like to buy jars of these chiles made into pastes; they are inexpensive to order online. You can also buy dried chiles that you then rehydrate in warm water, and if you are lucky, you can find them fresh-frozen in some stores.

CULANTRO (ALSO CALLED *RECAO*)

Culantro and cilantro are different herbs and serve different purposes. While cilantro is generally used fresh as a garnish or in raw condiments like salsas and guacamoles, culantro holds up much better to heat and is a cooking staple in many cuisines, including Puerto Rican. The flavor is somewhat similar to that of cilantro, but distinctively different. It is a very important component of the Puerto Rican cooking base Sofrito (page 148).

SOUR/BITTER ORANGES

The sour orange goes by many names, including bitter, marmalade, Seville or bigarade orange, and as the name implies, they are quite sour and bitter tasting. They're not sweet at all and aren't suitable for eating raw the way you do with navel or other sweet oranges. They tend to be a little uglier than their sweet counterparts, with more wrinkles/dimples on the surface.

You may be able to find sour oranges at your local Latin grocery store. They may be labeled as *"naranja agria."* But if you can't find them, you can substitute a mixture of sweet orange juice with lime juice, with an optional touch of grapefruit juice (see Mojo Criollo, page 154, for more info).

BACALAO

Bacalao is codfish that has been preserved by salting and drying. Growing up in the mountainous region of Puerto Rico, this was the only type of seafood that Milagros had access to, since it is non-perishable. *Bacalao* holds a special place in many Puerto Ricans' hearts, especially when it is mixed into batter and fried up as Bacalaítos (page 56). Look for *bacalao* in the refrigerated section in bags, in cans or sometimes in wooden boxes at room temperature near the fish counter. If you can't find it, you can substitute fresh cod but the texture is less dense.

CHAYOTES

Chayotes are a type of gourd that, in the southern United States (particularly Louisiana), are known as mirlitons. They are pear-shaped with a puckered end. The flesh has a delicate flavor reminiscent of the taste of summer squash. They are excellent boiled and stuffed with meat, as a great nightshade-free alternative to stuffed peppers.

PANELA

Panela is the term for unrefined whole cane sugar in Latin America. It is typically sold in blocks or cones of varying sizes, but sometimes you can find it grated and sold in bags. You can grate blocks of it by slicing thinly with a knife and chopping. It has a lovely deep, rich, almost caramel-like flavor. If you can't find it, coconut sugar makes a good substitute.

HUACATAY (BLACK MINT)

The herb *huacatay*, also called black mint, is a staple in Peruvian cuisine. You can find it sold as a paste in jars in stores as well as online. It has a unique flavor that is hard to replicate exactly, but a blend of about 2 parts mint, 2 parts cilantro and 1 part basil will work. To make a paste, add the herbs to a food processor or blender with a little extra-virgin olive oil, then divide into portions in an ice cube tray (just as with the Sofrito, page 148). But I recommend ordering a jar of the real thing at least once so you can experience the true flavor.

A FEW NOTES ON PALEO INGREDIENTS

MEATS

The Paleo diet encourages us to source the best-raised meats we can. This means for beef and lamb to seek out grass-fed and grass-finished if it is available and can fit your budget. Pasture-raised but grain-finished is the next-best option. For chicken, look for pasture-raised birds (free range is not the same thing.) Pork is also ideally pasture-raised. The tides are changing in the farming industry, and you are now able to find grass-fed and pasture-raised meats at large national retailers, such as Target and Aldi. You may also have local farmers who sell at farmers' markets or in bulk. The website EatWild.com is a good place to search for local producers. It can be well worth the investment in a chest freezer to be able to buy one-quarter of grass-fed cow or half of a pastured pig in bulk for a very low price per pound to feed you for months.

If you are unable to source these kinds of meats locally, you have several options for ordering online. If they do not fit into your budget please don't feel shame and just do the best that you can do. I personally think that it is better to spend a little more on well-raised meats and then to cut corners with produce, buying conventional (non-organic) to save money.

RED PALM OIL

There is a misconception in the Paleo community that the sourcing of all red palm oil harms orangutans. This is simply not true, especially if you buy a brand produced in South America. Orangutans do not even live in South America! There are several brands with transparent sourcing practices that are eco-friendly and sustainable. I use Nutiva brand.

PALM SHORTENING

A few recipes call for palm shortening. As mentioned earlier, be sure to choose a brand that uses eco-friendly and substainable practices. I use the Nutiva brand.

EXTRA-VIRGIN OLIVE OIL

Somehow a myth got started in the Paleo community that extra-virgin olive oil is dangerous to cook with and that it should be used only for cold applications, such as salad dressing. This is simply not true and has been thoroughly debunked. Extra-virgin olive oil is excellent for many of the dishes in this cookbook and is a traditionally used fat in these cuisines.

LARD

This ingredient could just as easily be put into the traditional Latin ingredients section. When buying lard, never, ever choose the hydrogenated version, which you will find on the shelves of the store rather than in the refrigerated section. This shelf-stable lard is full of dangerous and extremely unhealthy trans fats. Instead, choose freshly rendered lard in the refrigerated section and sometimes the freezer section. There are also quite a few sources you can order from online now. Or you can render it yourself at home from pork fat. I buy mine rendered and frozen from a local pasture-based farmer.

UNREFINED SALT

We now know that refined white table salt is not a healthy part of our diet, but luckily there are many options now for whole, unrefined salts that contain vital trace minerals. I like to use a finely ground pink Himalayan salt to cook with and a coarse gray Celtic sea salt for garnishing dishes.

ACKNOWLEDGMENTS

First and foremost, I would like to thank my husband and soul mate, Andy. Without your unwavering support there is no way I would have survived the cookbook writing process. You have always been my number one fan (okay, I think Mom might have earned that title, but now it's you!) and encouraged me to carry on even when I'm feeling overwhelmed or not good enough. Thank you for never letting me give up.

To Milagros, my sweet mother-in-law, thank you so much for taking me under your wing and teaching me your family recipes. You have always been so patient with me when I ask a million questions, and it was such a joy to work with you on immortalizing your family recipes in this cookbook.

To Jennifer Robins, this book would not have happened without you! Thank you for your encouragement to write it and for the introduction to Page Street. It has been an honor to call you my friend and be inspired by your successes.

To Kelly Bejelly, my blogging mentor, thank you for always believing in me and forcing me to venture outside of my comfort zone as a blogger and recipe developer. You helped me take myself seriously as a businesswoman. Thank you so much for your support over the years!

To Jessica Espinoza, my longtime blogging friend, I am so grateful for our friendship and for all of the encouragement and advice you have given me over the years.

To Mike Falcone, my acupuncturist, thank you for teaching me to truly value self-care, sharing your knowledge about meditation and for taking such great care of both me and Andy. Thank you for helping me to manage my stress, stay healthy and keep my sanity while writing this book—I might not have finished it, otherwise!

To Davina, my big sister, thank you for always believing in me, for being full of ideas when I need advice, and ready to help if I'm working on a tough recipe.

To Dad and Leanne, thank you so much for always being so incredibly loving and supportive.

To my readers and fans, thank you so much for your encouragement and enthusiasm as I worked on this project. Y'all really are the best!

To Page Street Publishing, thank you for believing in me and allowing me to bring this labor of love into the world. It is a dream come true to share these recipes with such a wide audience.

And finally, Mom, I wish you were still here to see this cookbook. I know you would be so proud! Thank you for teaching me never to give up on my dreams, and for never letting me believe I wasn't smart enough or talented enough to do anything I put my mind to.

ABOUT THE AUTHORS

AMANDA TORRES, a scientist by training with an MS in neuroscience, is passionate about sharing good food and information to empower others to reclaim good health. She blogs at The Curious Coconut, where she shares her most delicious Paleo and autoimmune protocol (AIP) recipes with a dash of science on the side.

She experienced the healing power of food when she first went Paleo in 2010, after failing to lose weight following conventional advice and facing extremely poor health and a long list of scary health problems. By one year on the Paleo diet she had lost 80 pounds and reversed prediabetes, hypertension, metabolic syndrome, rosacea, dyslipidemia and depression. This lifestyle has also kept her autoimmune skin condition hidradenitis suppurativa mostly in remission.

She also loves sharing information about mindfulness, meditation and Chinese medicine with her audience, since she has found these tried-and-true ancient tools to be the key to a well-rounded healthy lifestyle.

When she is not developing recipes, you can find her playing with her three cats and Chihuahua, tending to her backyard garden, taking in the culture of her beloved city of Memphis and beating her husband at video games.

MILAGROS TORRES was born in Arecibo, Puerto Rico, in 1940, in the barrio of Sabana Hoyos in the mountains. Arecibo is famous for its Observatory, and is located on the northern side of the island. Generations of Milagros's family have settled and lived in the barrio of Sabana Hoyos. Even today, this area is remote, with only a few narrow roads winding up into this mountain region, with many still living off the land on small farms.

Milagros learned to cook from her mother, who raised her children as a single working mother, when she was only ten years old. She started simply with learning how to cook white rice, but was soon helping to prepare the family meals because her mother worked long hours to support her and her younger brothers.

These cooking traditions and family recipes that have been passed down for generations have carried her through her whole life. She has always taken great pride in her home cooking and raised her three sons on the same traditional foods she grew up eating. She takes great pleasure in cooking for her growing family.

In 2010, after seeing the health improvements in her son Andy and daughter-in-law Amanda, she adopted a gluten-free diet that healed her acid reflux and other digestive discomfort.

INDEX